Steve Sandberg was born in the Bronx, New York in 1945 and his family moved to California and back. He became a special education teacher in a Brooklyn school and after witnessing the World Trade Center collapse decided to illustrate his first book, *A Day of Infamy Revisited.* Steve appeared in a Pocono Newspaper and later made appearances at libraries and schools including Rocky Point Middle School. Now retired, Steve's journey into his creation of 9/11 visualizations ended in 2023.

Steve Sandberg

A Day of Infamy Revisited

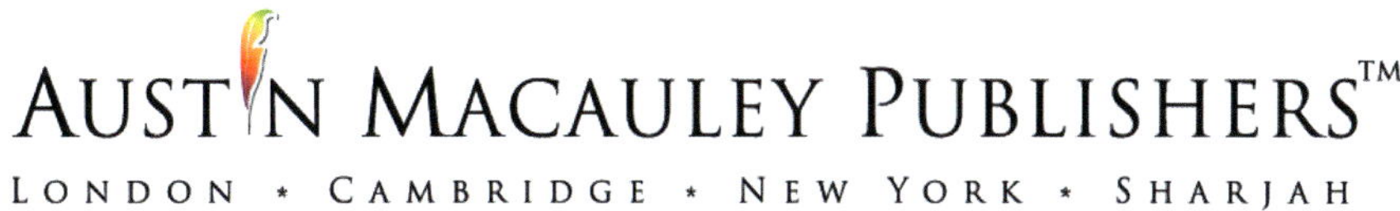

AUSTIN MACAULEY PUBLISHERS™

LONDON ★ CAMBRIDGE ★ NEW YORK ★ SHARJAH

Ordering Information
Quantity sales: Special discounts are available on quantity purchases by corporations, associations, and others. For details, contact the publisher at the address below.

Publisher's Cataloging-in-Publication data
Sandberg, Steve
A Day of Infamy Revisited

ISBN 9798891559011 (Paperback)
ISBN 9798891559028 (Hardback)
ISBN 9798891559035 (ePub e-book)

Library of Congress Control Number: 2024912014

www.austinmacauley.com/us

First Published 2024
Austin Macauley Publishers LLC
40 Wall Street, 33rd Floor, Suite 3302
New York, NY 10005
USA

mail-usa@austinmacauley.com
+1 (646) 5125767

Dedications

This work has spanned more than 20 years and is dedicated to the memory of all those who perished on that September day and to the heroic fire, police, and healthcare providers who worked tirelessly at the World Trade Center site.

Acknowledgments

Special personal acknowledgment and dedication are also noted to the memory of Hildegard Kroeger, library curator at North Shore Public Library, and to my wife, Barbara, for her unrelenting support and belief.

To North Shore Public Library, Comsewogue Public Library, and Rocky Point Middle School.

Artist's Statement

Like a composer may use a leitmotif (recurring theme) in a symphony's development, the use of 9 and/or 11 numbered characters by this artist, play a prominent role in the generation of many of the enclosed images. The power and scope of that life-altering day still remains as vivid years later, to this day.

Tragic events can often be the catalyst and inspiration for the creation of meaningful works of art. In this case, it was the Sept. 11 catastrophe of 2001 which provided the stimulus that would ultimately lead me down a totally unforeseen path; revealing an aptitude never previously observed. Other than a proclivity for drawing geometric shapes, no artistic tendencies had even been evident.

People who have explored "my world" have seen different things. Take the journey and see what you can uncover. Remember, in the future, be open to the feasibility that sometimes unexpected abilities can appear anytime in one's life. Be ready to embrace the opportunity these possibilities present and take them down your own personal road of discovery.

Table of Contents

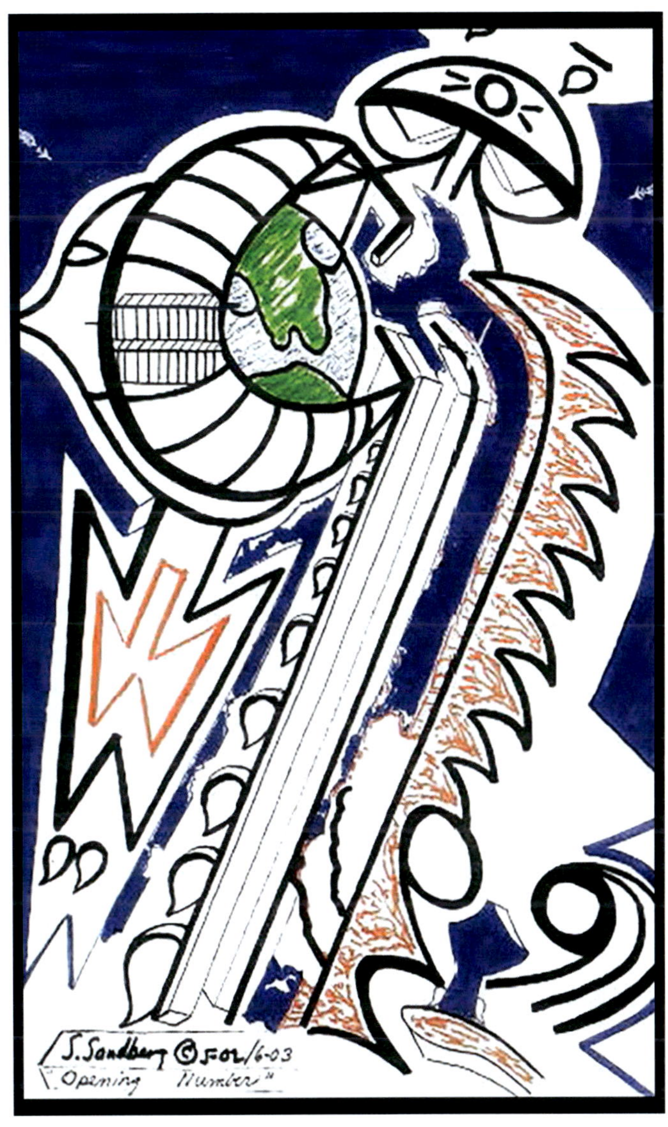

Opening Number

In a strife torn world, a cacophonic refrain shatters a beautiful Tuesday morning.

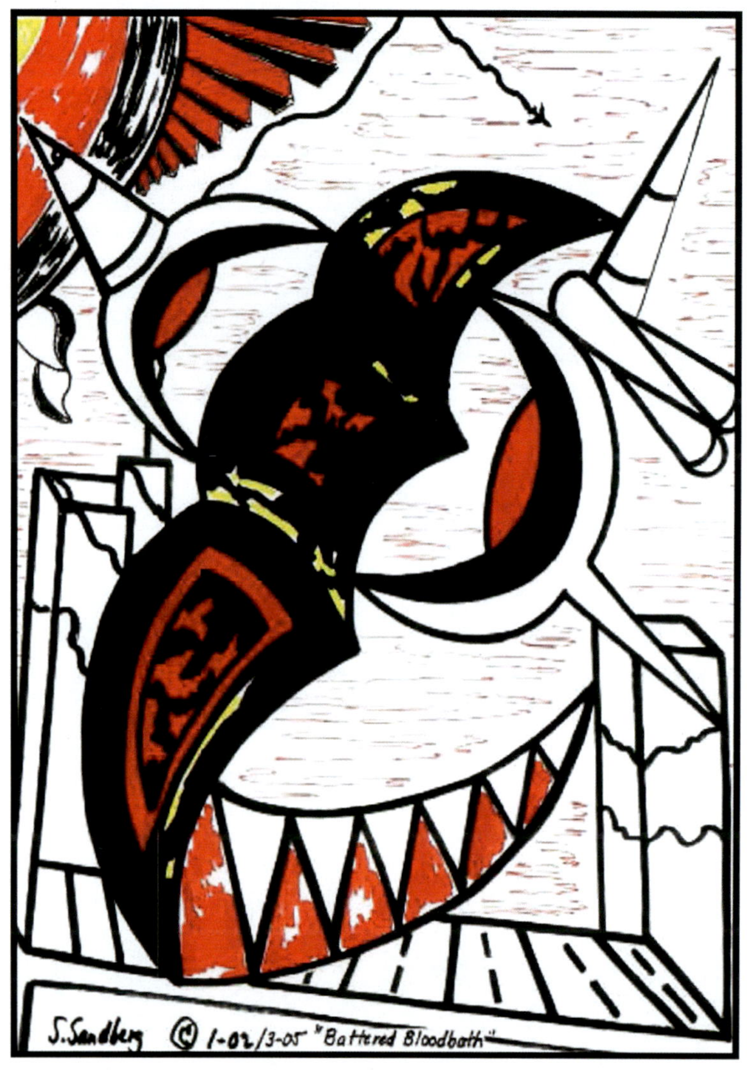

Battered Bloodbath

The ultimate of hostility soared from the skies, targeting
the innocent.

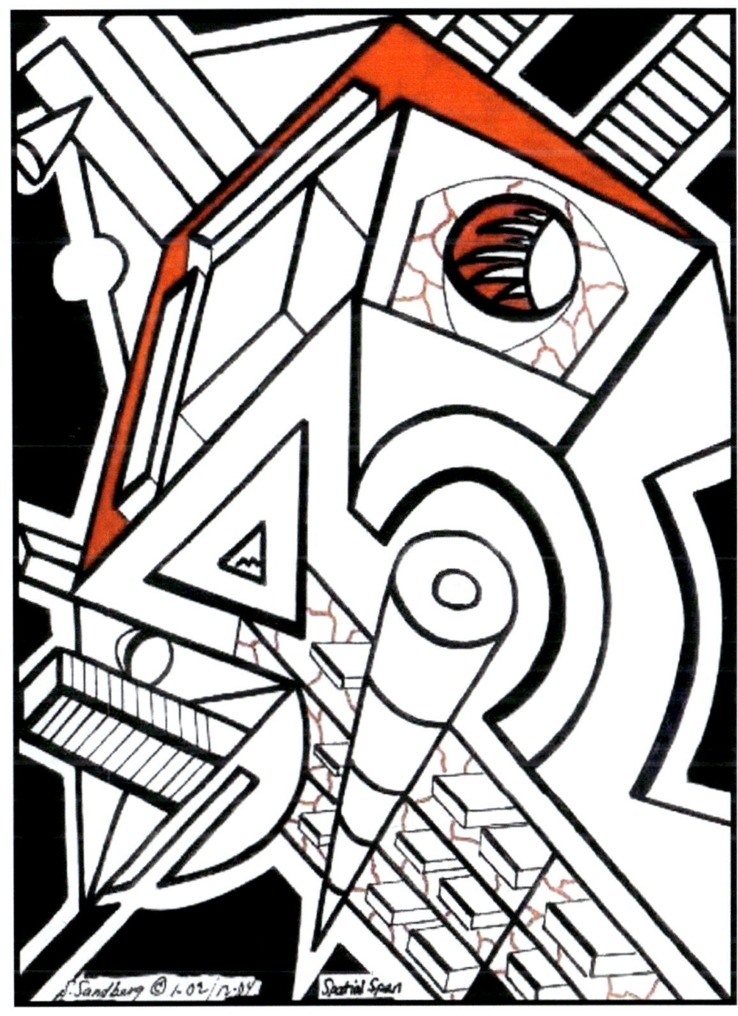

Spatial Span

An abstract view is evident from above the clouds where clarity
on human discourse is often more objective.

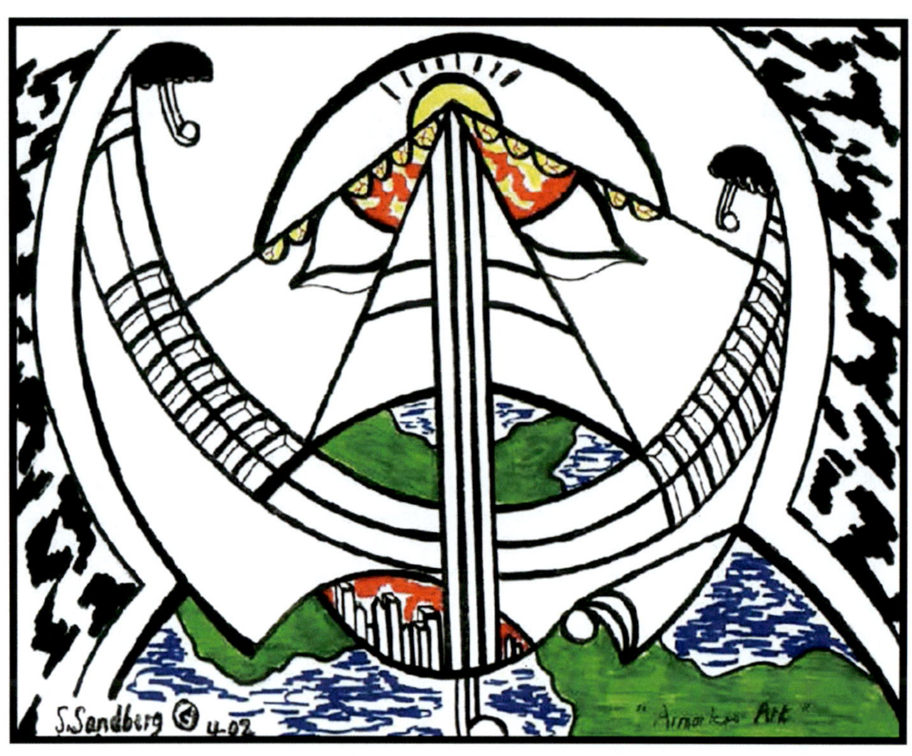

Armorless Ark

The ship of state, for an instant in time, appeared rudderless
and unprepared.

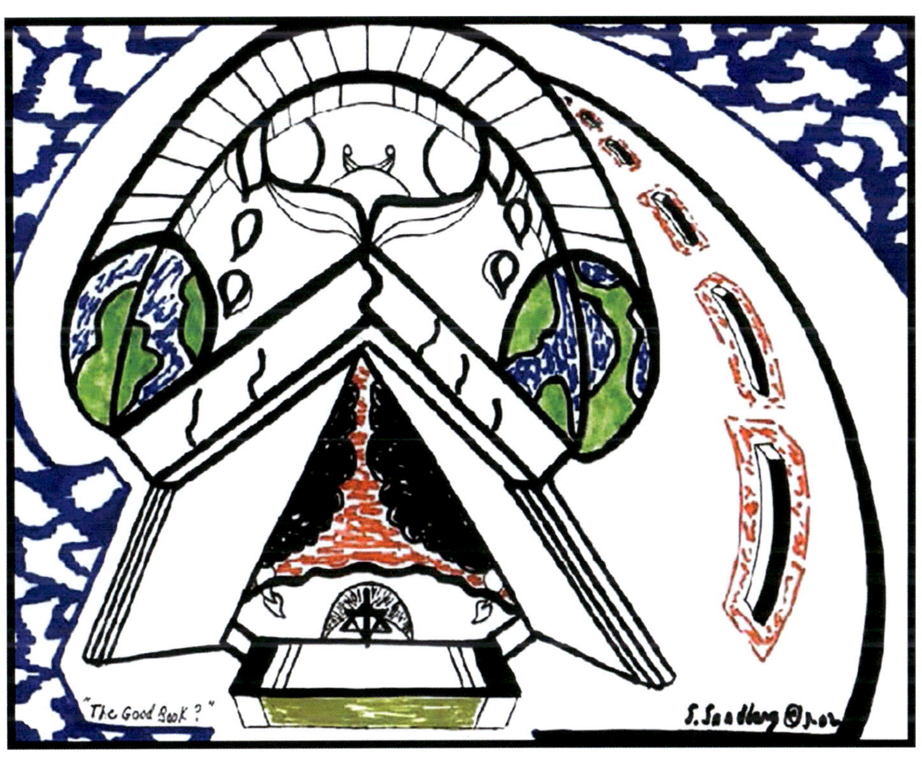

The Good Book?

Religion is often twisted and exploited to damaging affect against those deemed to be non-believers.

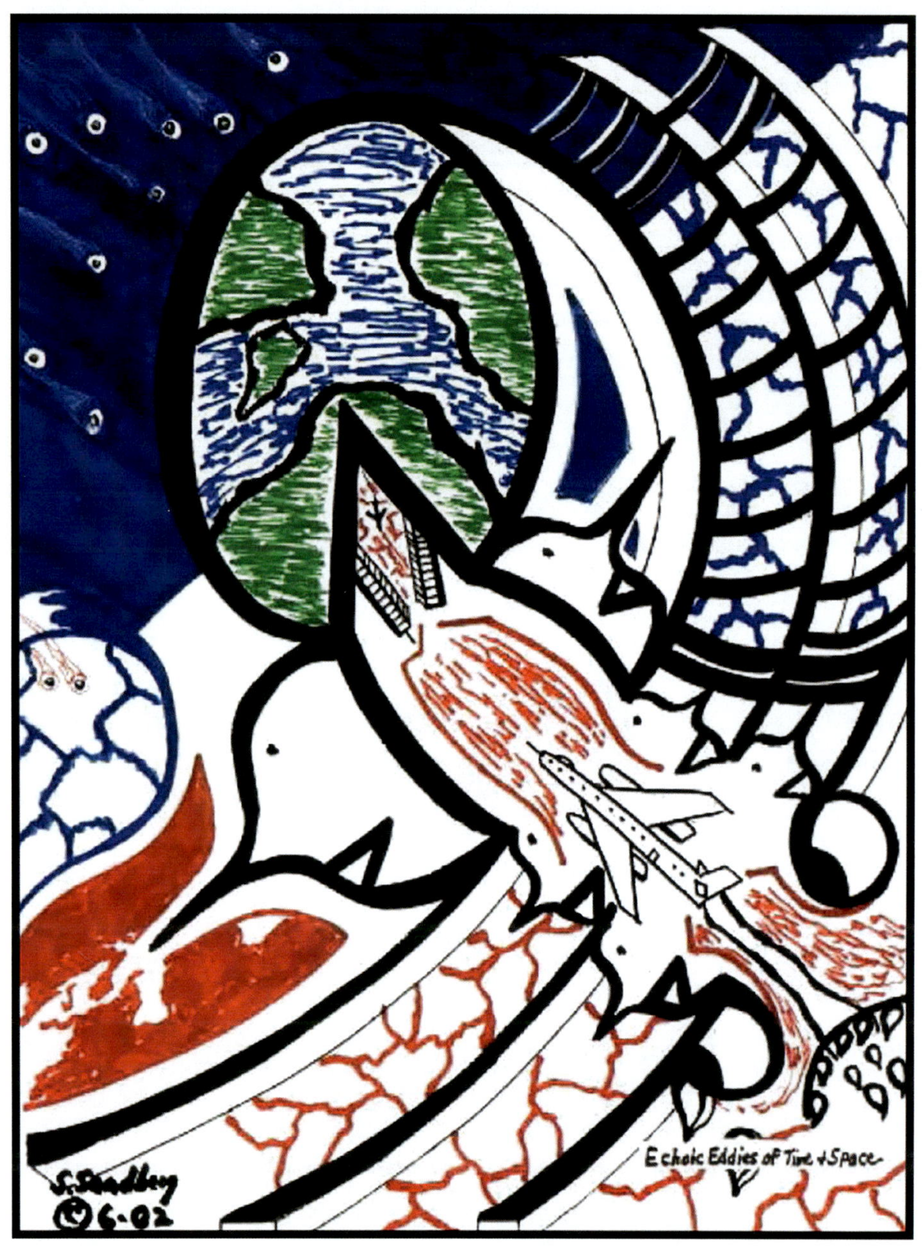

Echoic Eddies of Time and Space

A moment in the past will forever-linger, linger…

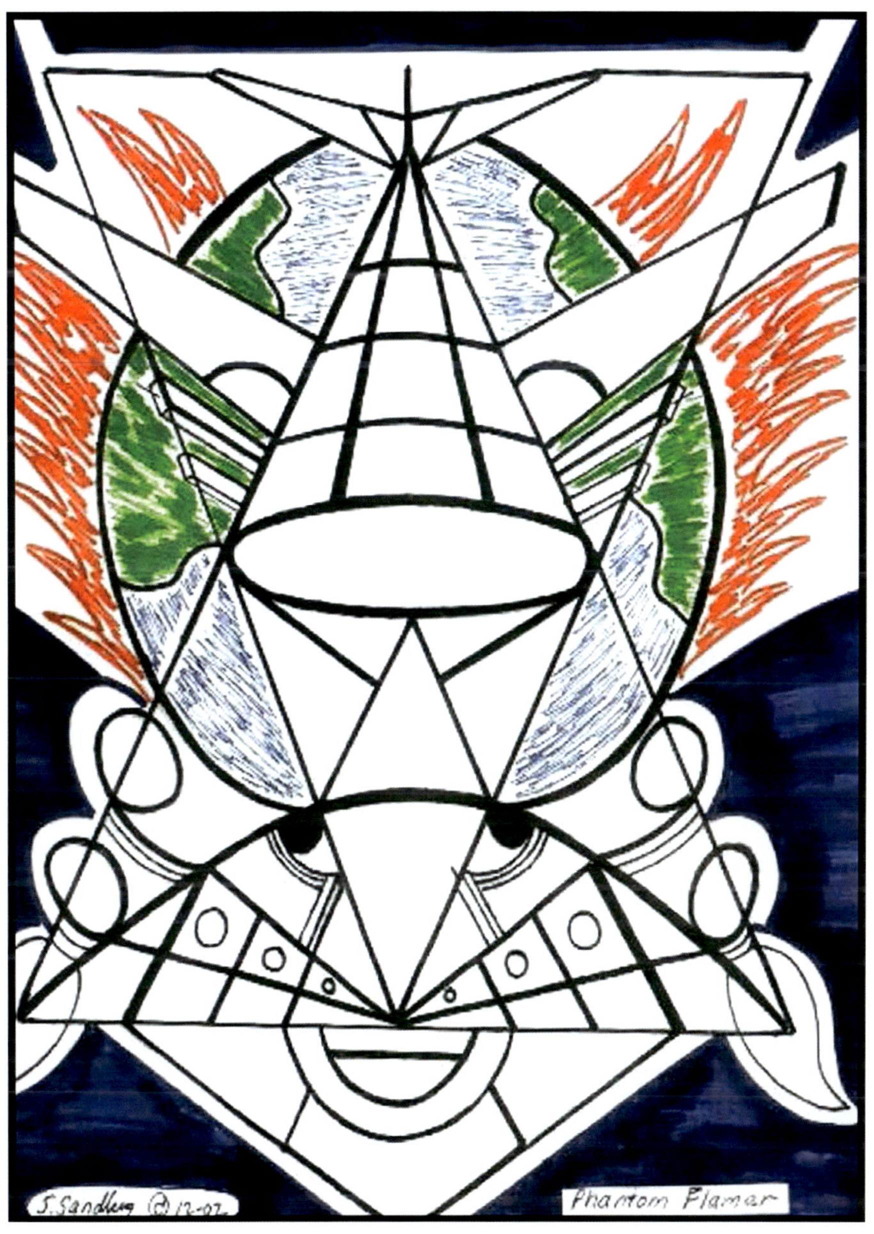

Phantom Flamer

The Face of Evil brought disorder and destruction in its wake.

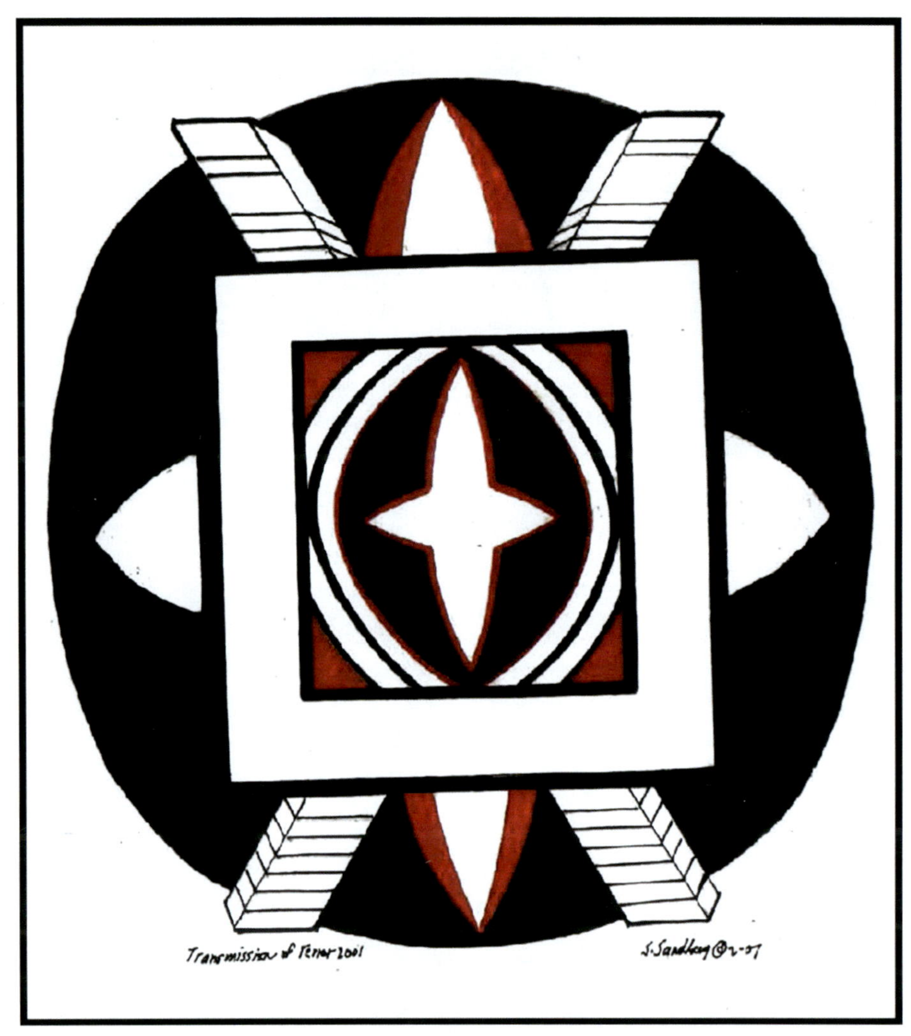

Transmission of Terror

A timeless broadcast vibrating across the airwaves.

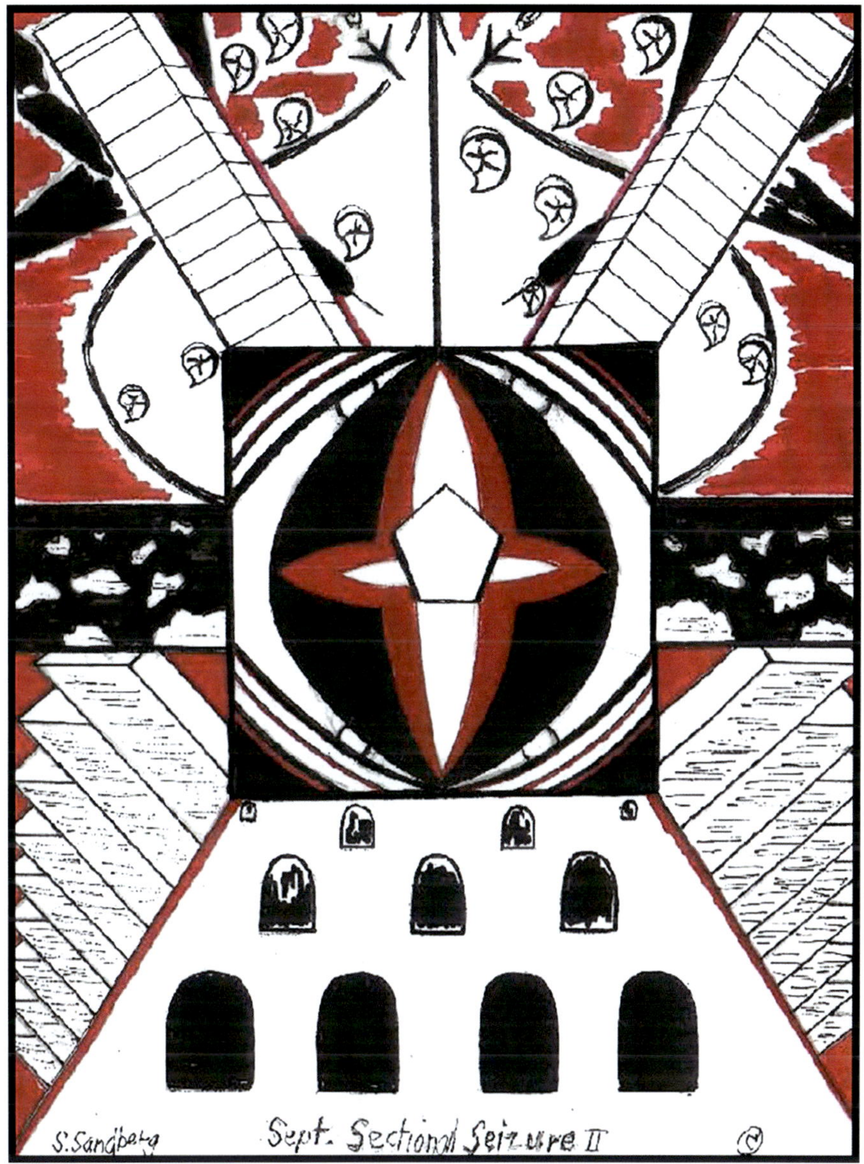

September Sectional Seizure

Snapshot views of the paralyzing nature of the transpired events.

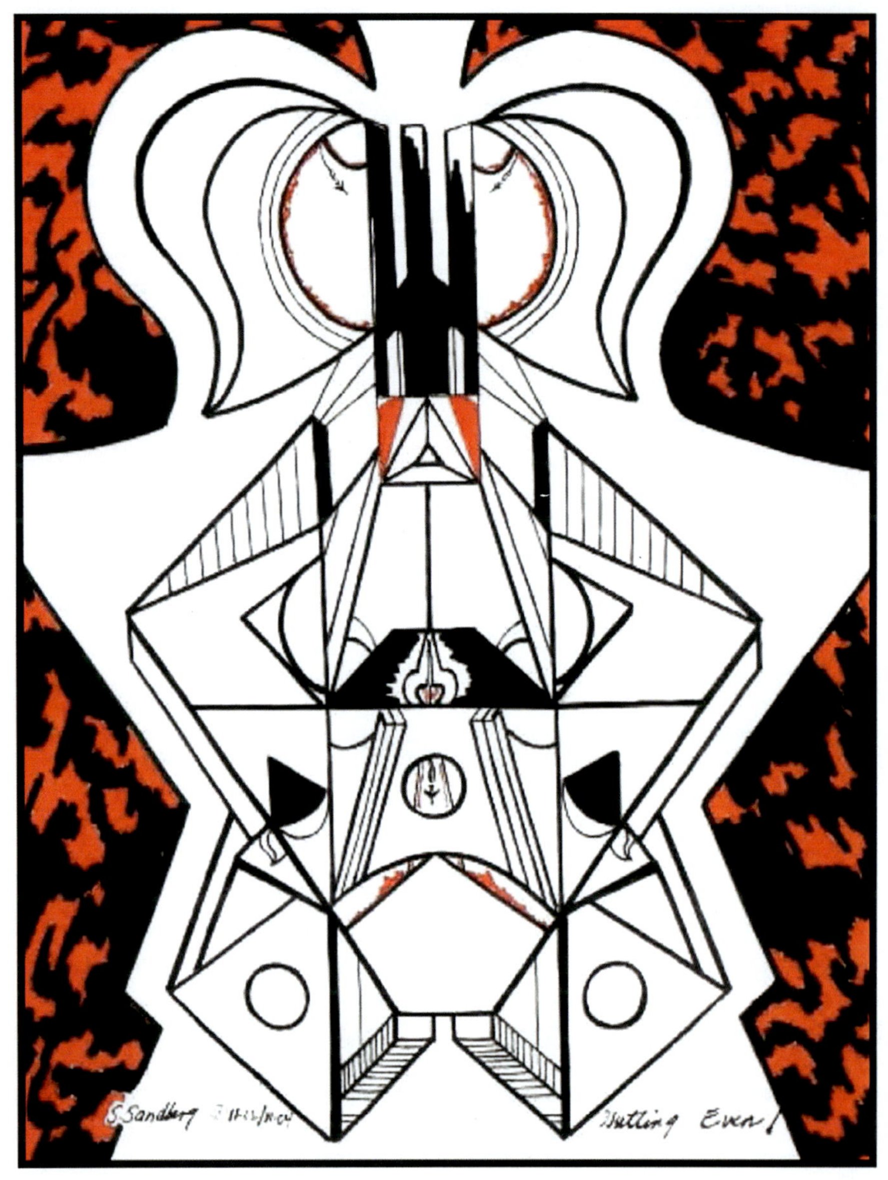

Getting Even!

They were bent on getting 'even' – they DID!

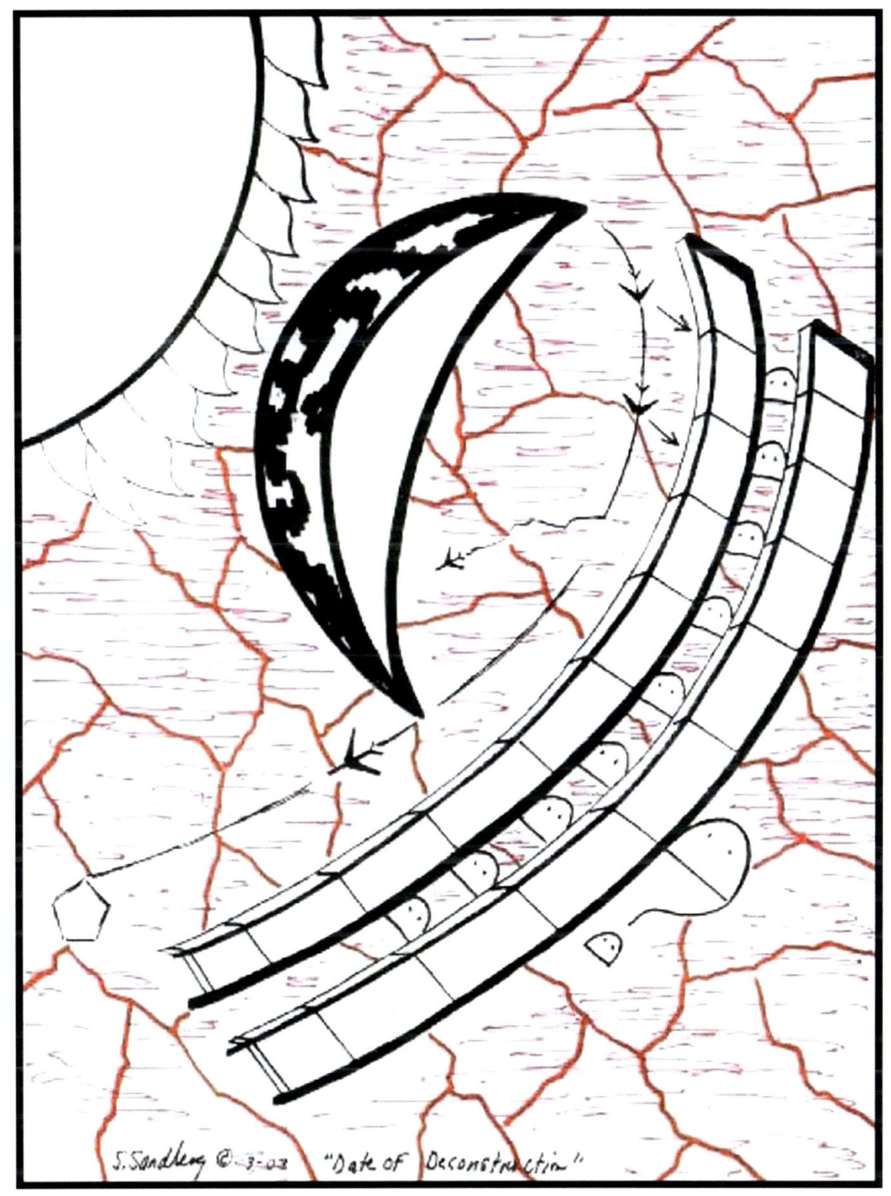

Date of Deconstruction

A date, like December 7th, that will be engrained in the human psyche.

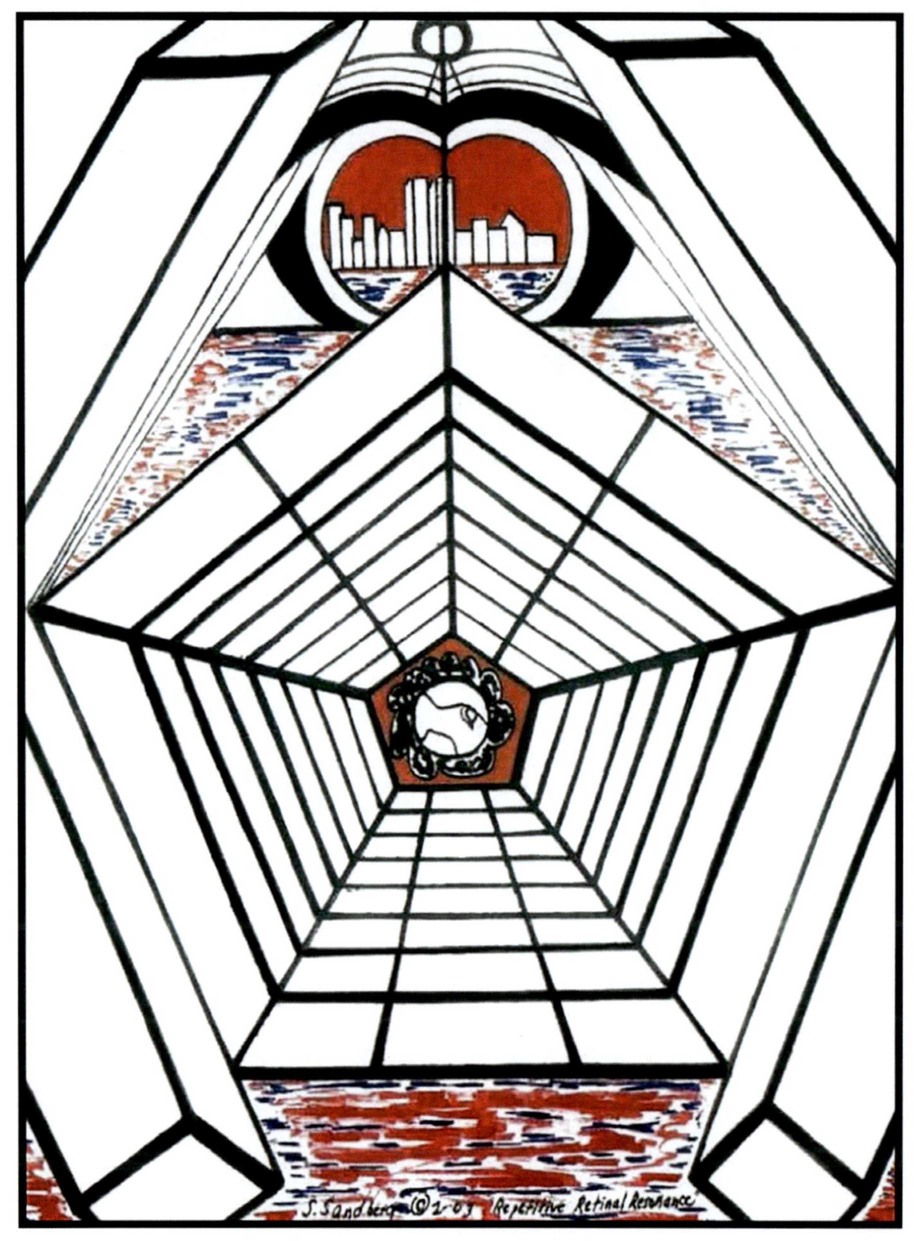

Repetitive Retinal Resonance

Receiver of the 'image', over and over again.

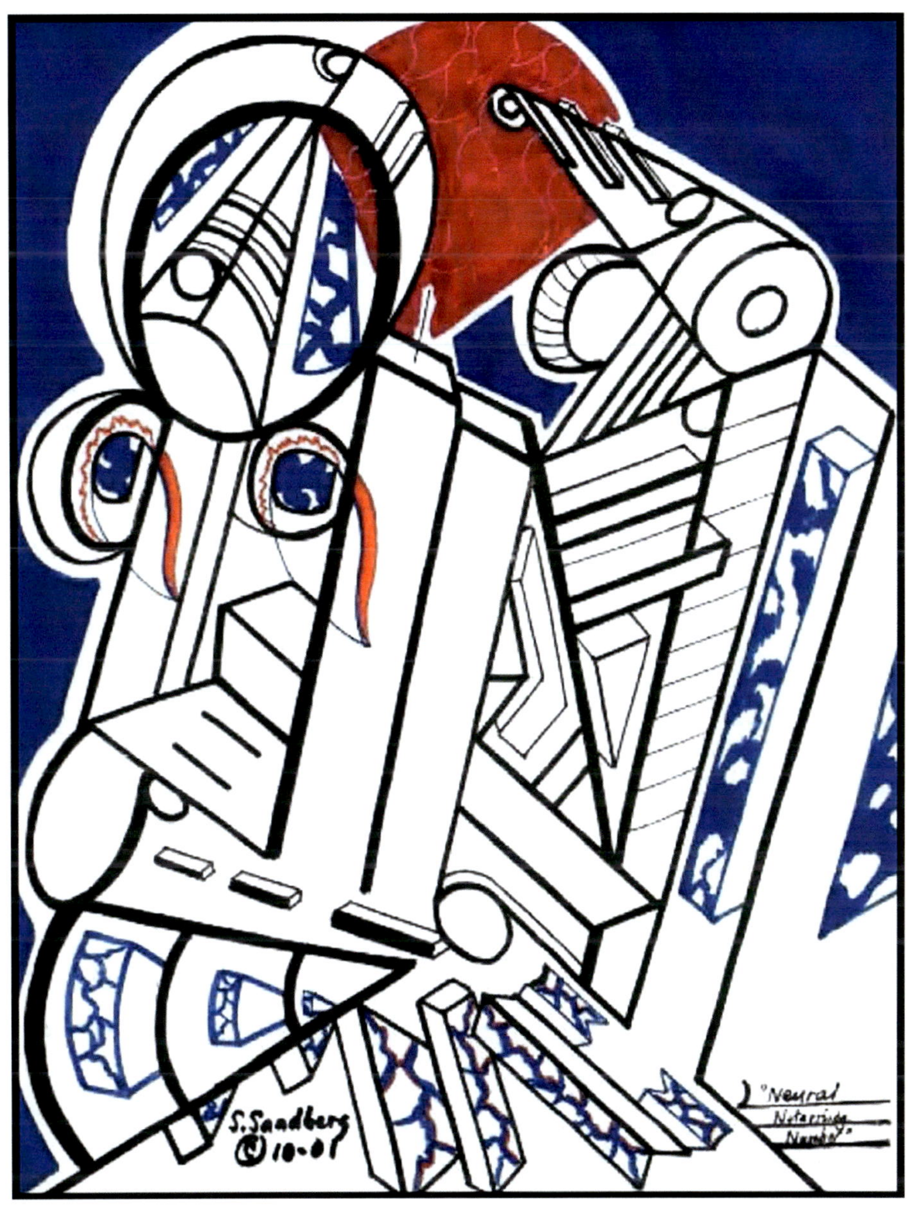

Neural Notarizing Number

A Calendar date that has struck at the heart of the American
Nervous System.

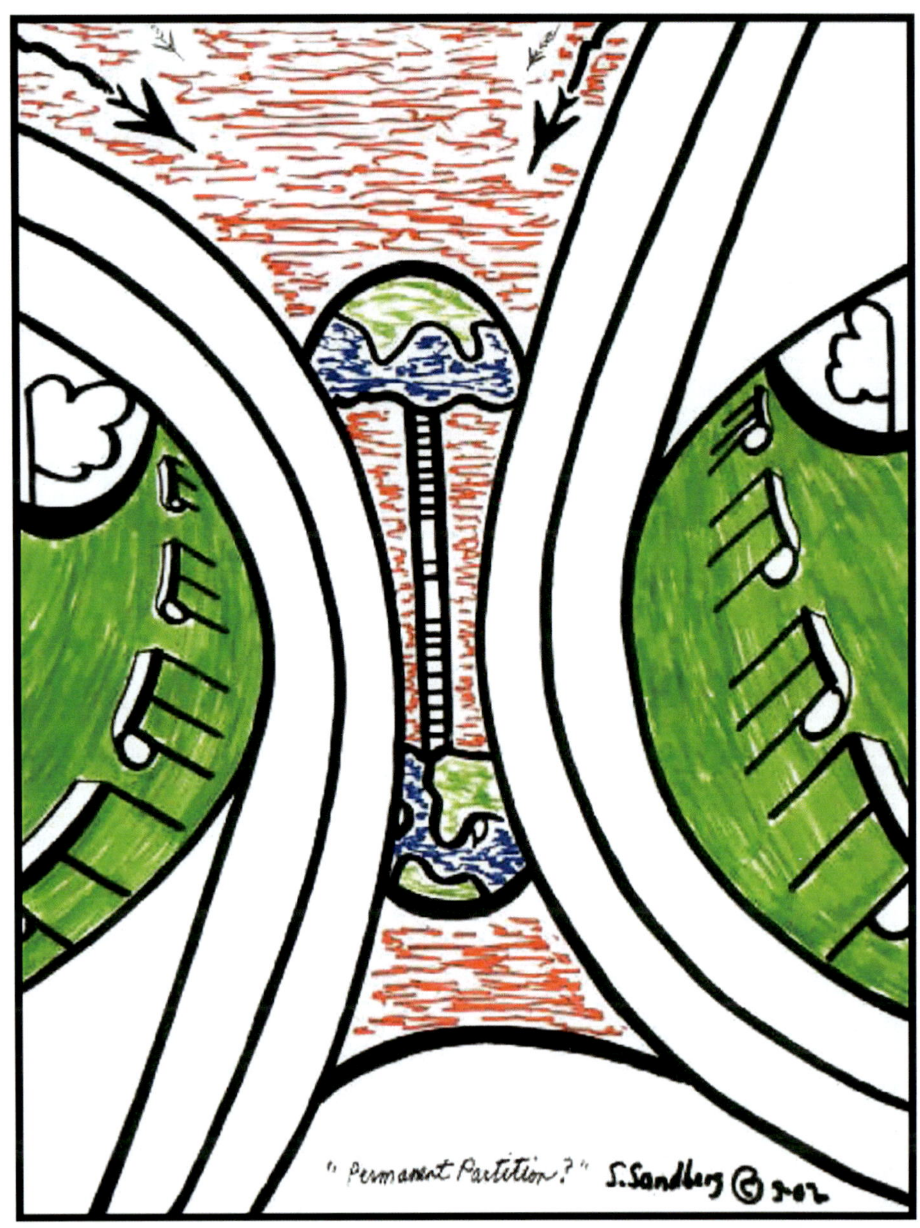

Permanent Partition

Governments 'Play the game' and try to consolidate
their power by blaming others for their internal difficulties.

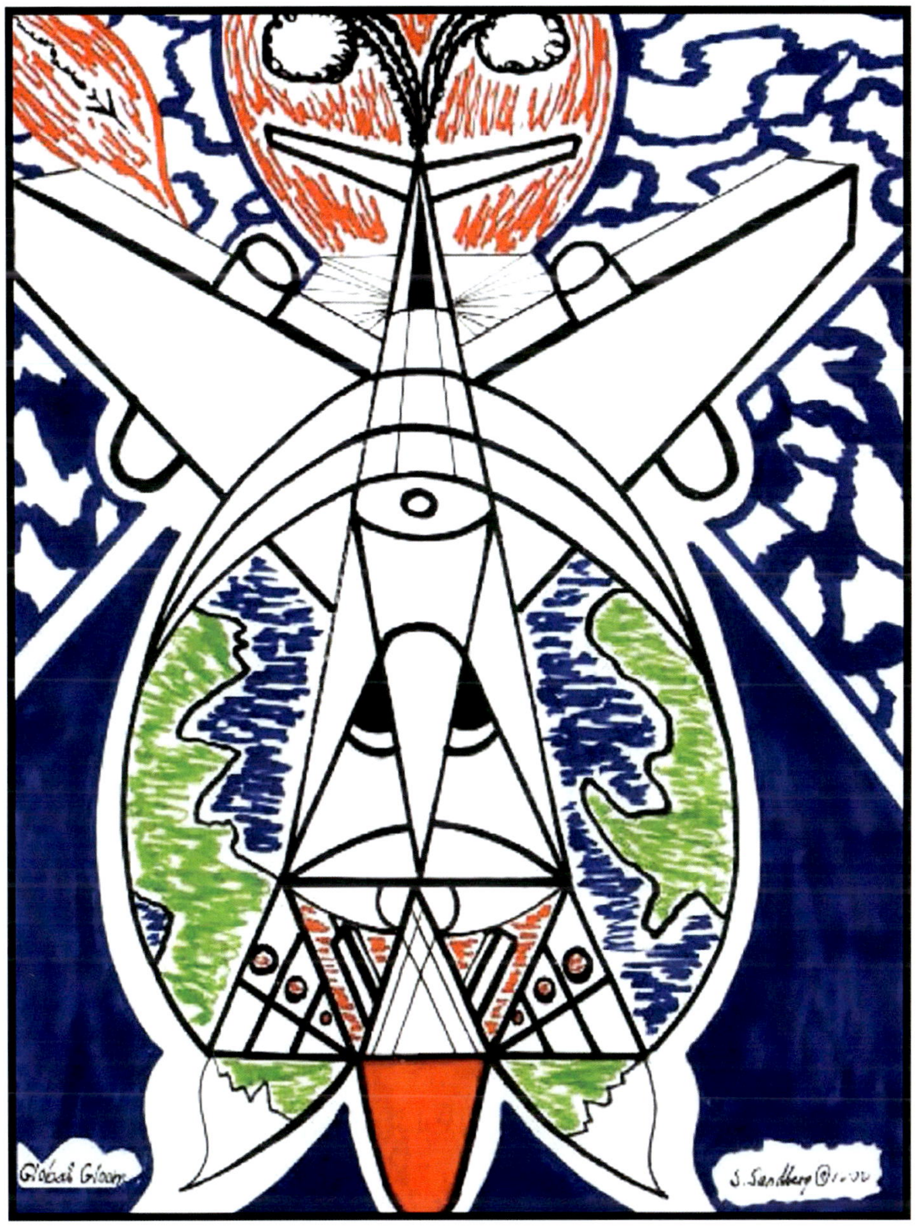

Global Gloom

It was man's great early 20th Century creation that would ultimately be used as a masked vehicle of destruction.

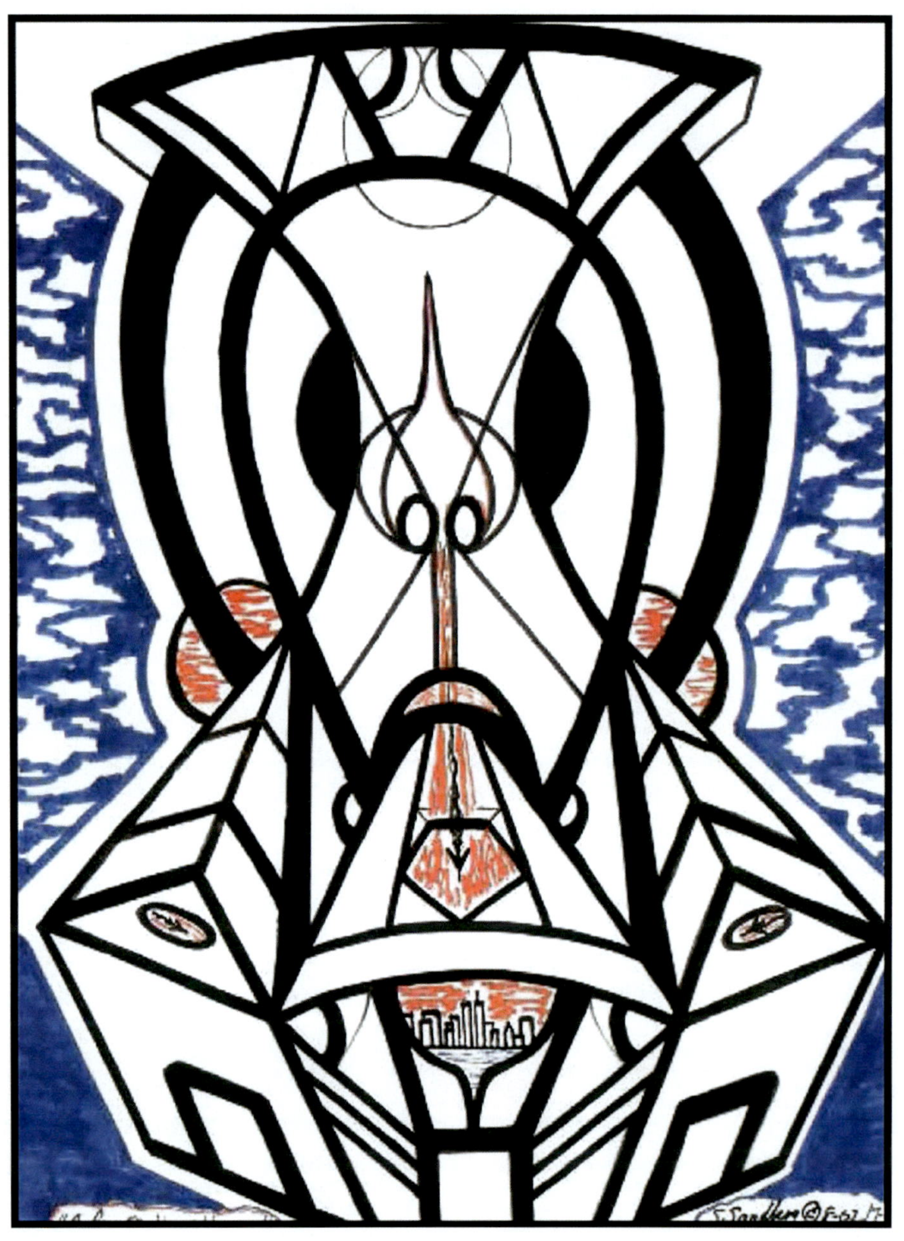

A Pox on Your Houses!

Al Qaeda agents morph their Holy Book to justify their actions against the 'Nation of Satan'.

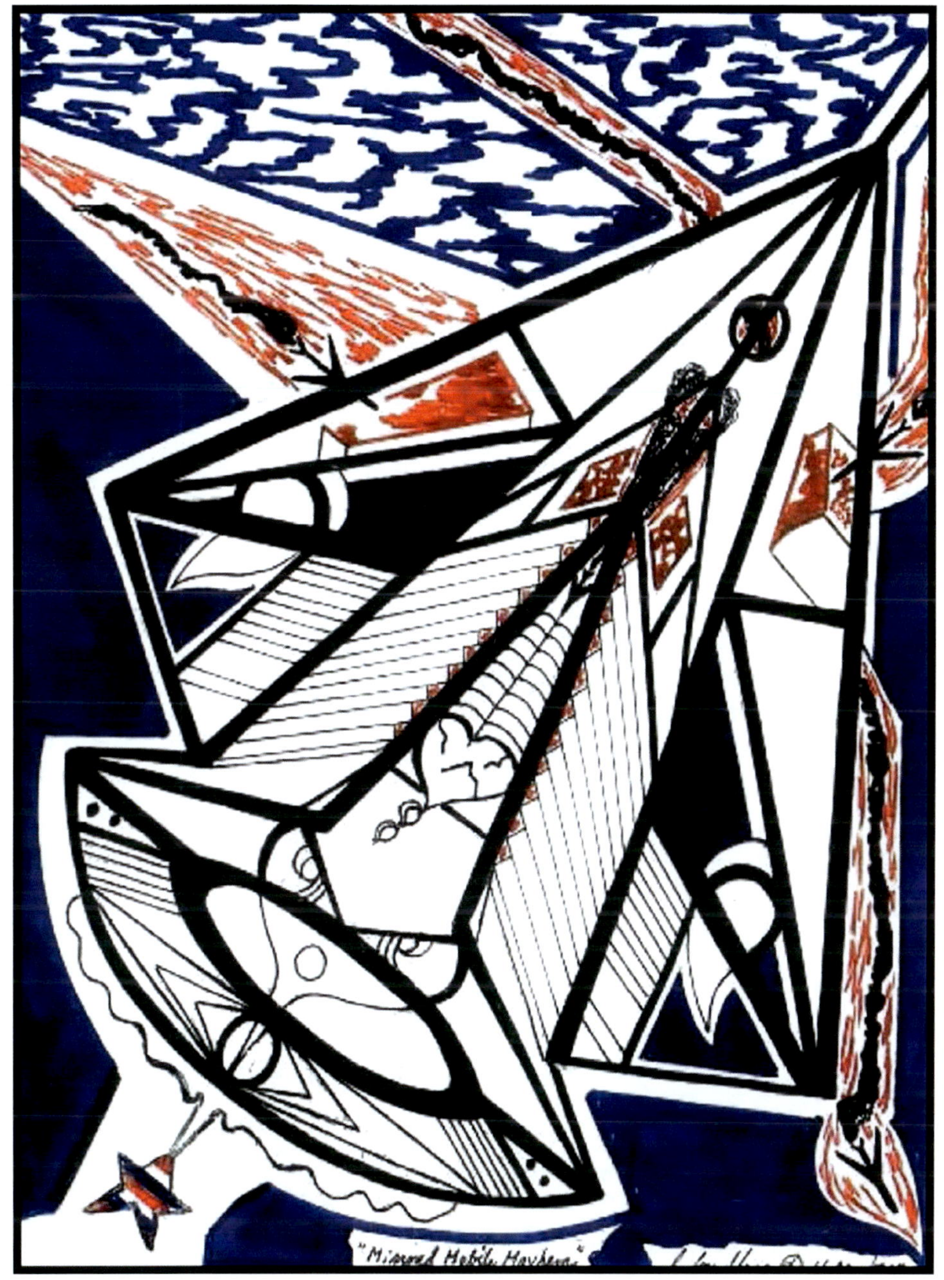

Mirrored Mobile Mayhem

A reflection on the flowing events and impending doom about to ensue.

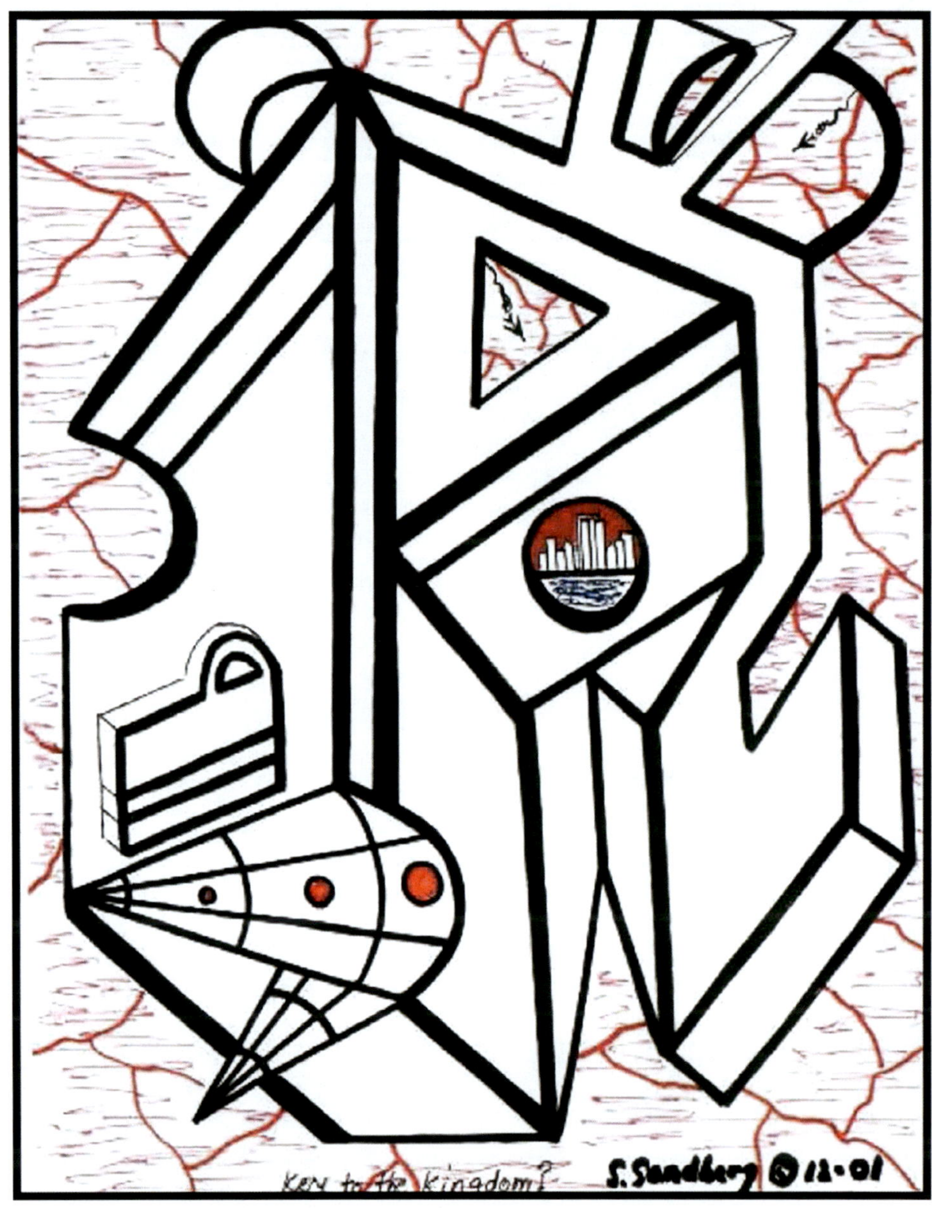

Key to the Kingdom?

To unlock the door of internal American security, these strikes would be necessary

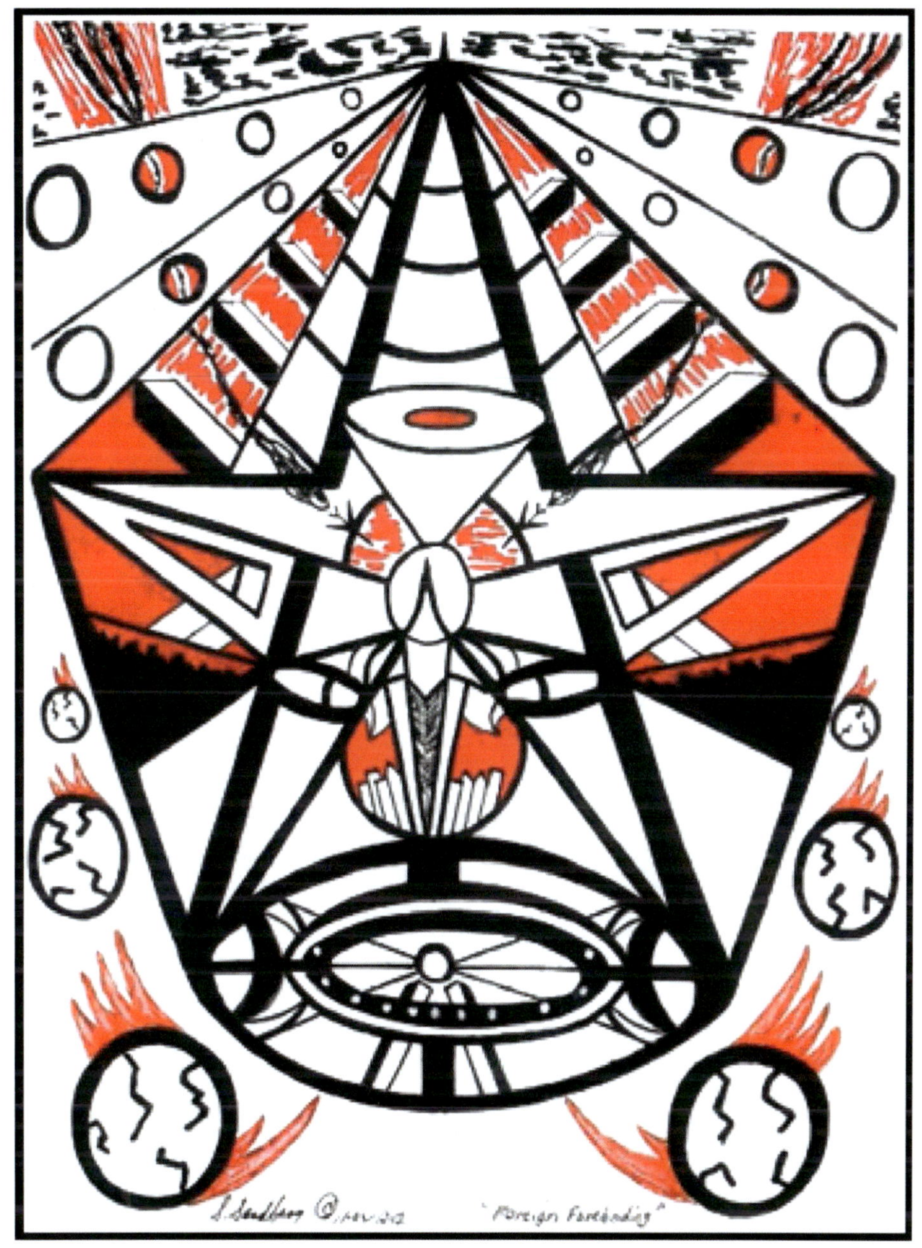

Foreign Foreboding

Faces, Tears, Flames and Fears!

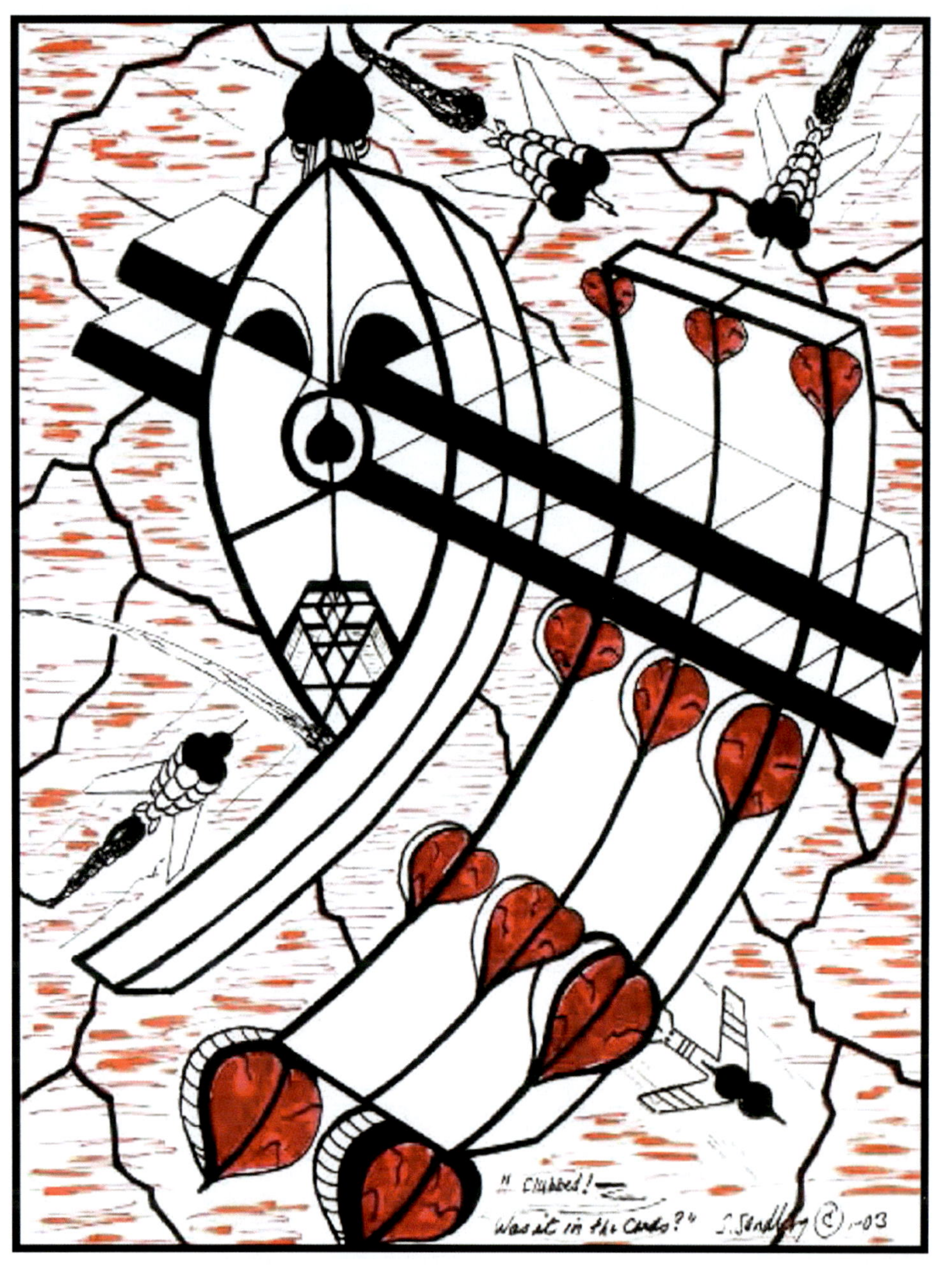

Clubbed!

Were circumstances such that 'the event' was in the cards?

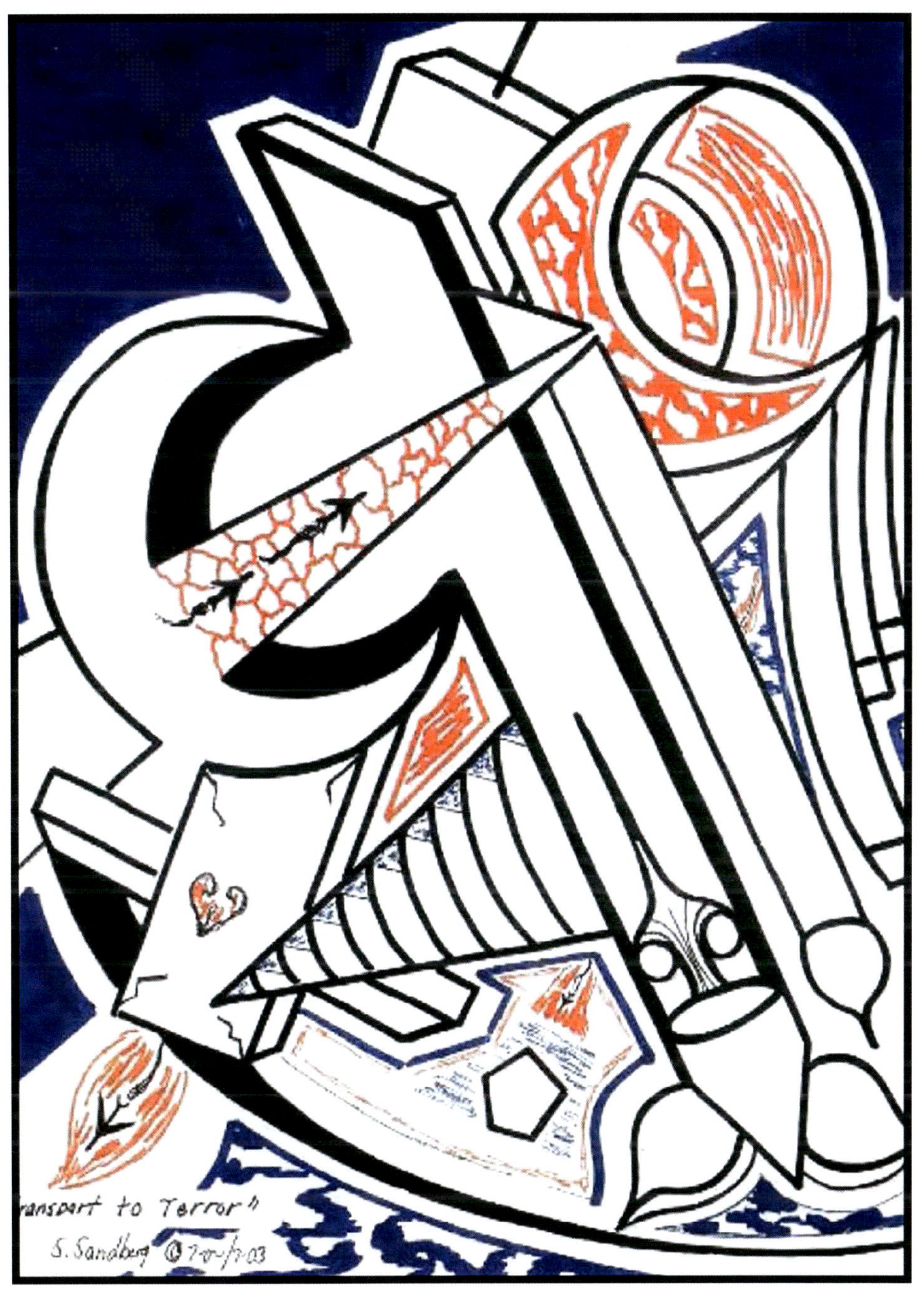

Transport to Terror

Perceived routine flights end in unspeakable horror.

The World Seemed

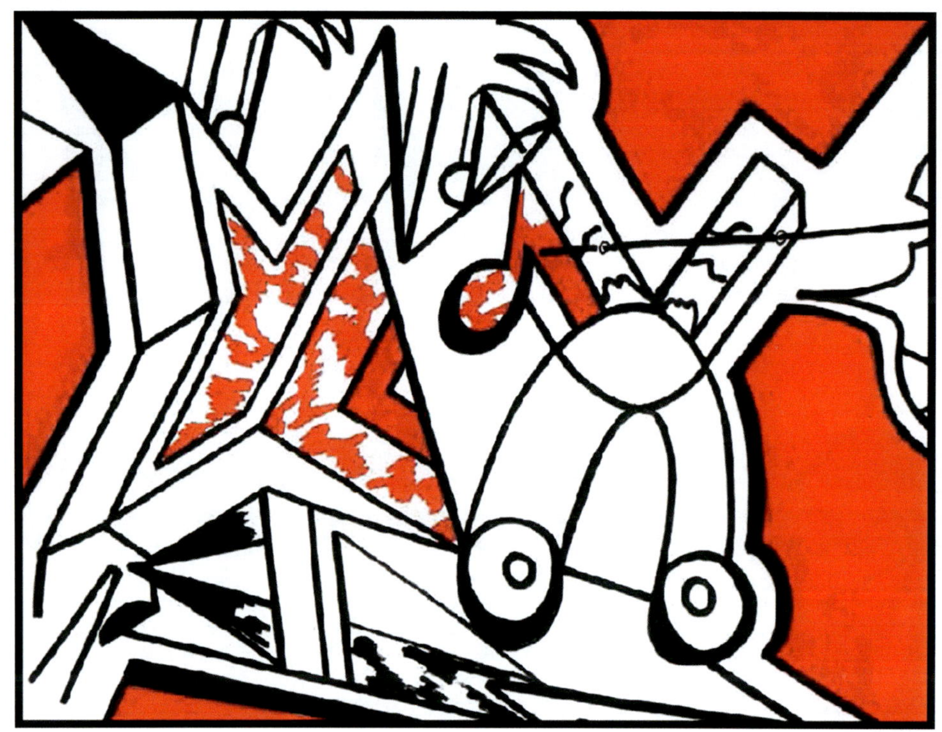

What's up? It's all in the View

Justice in the eyes of one segment of society is…

Tossed Upside Down

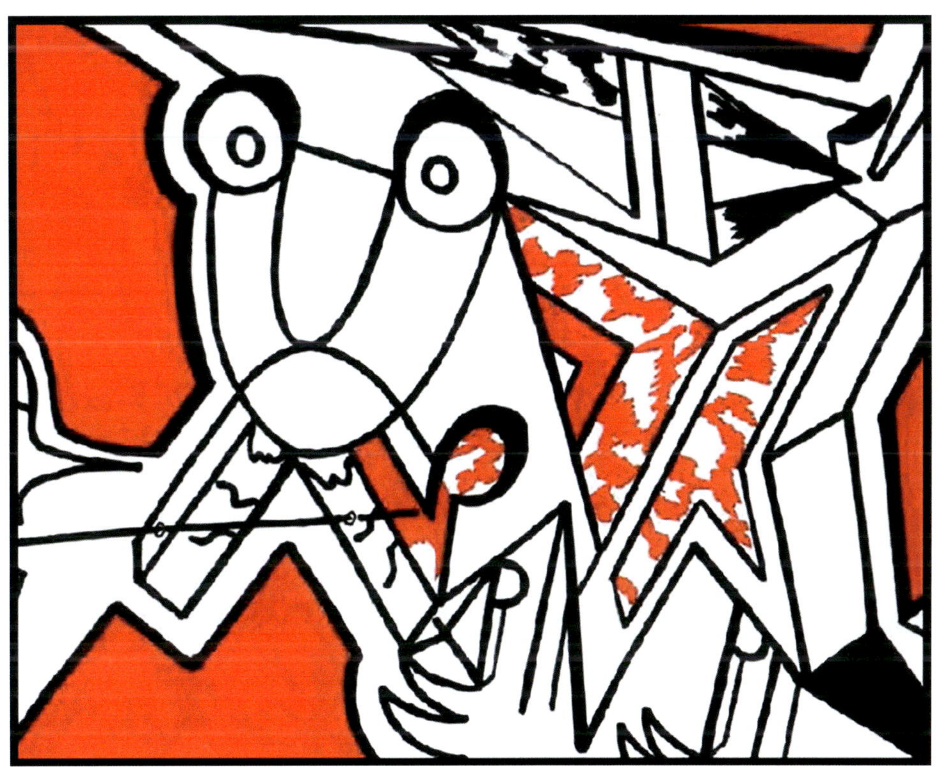

What's up? It's all in the View

Often perceived as injustice in the eyes of another.

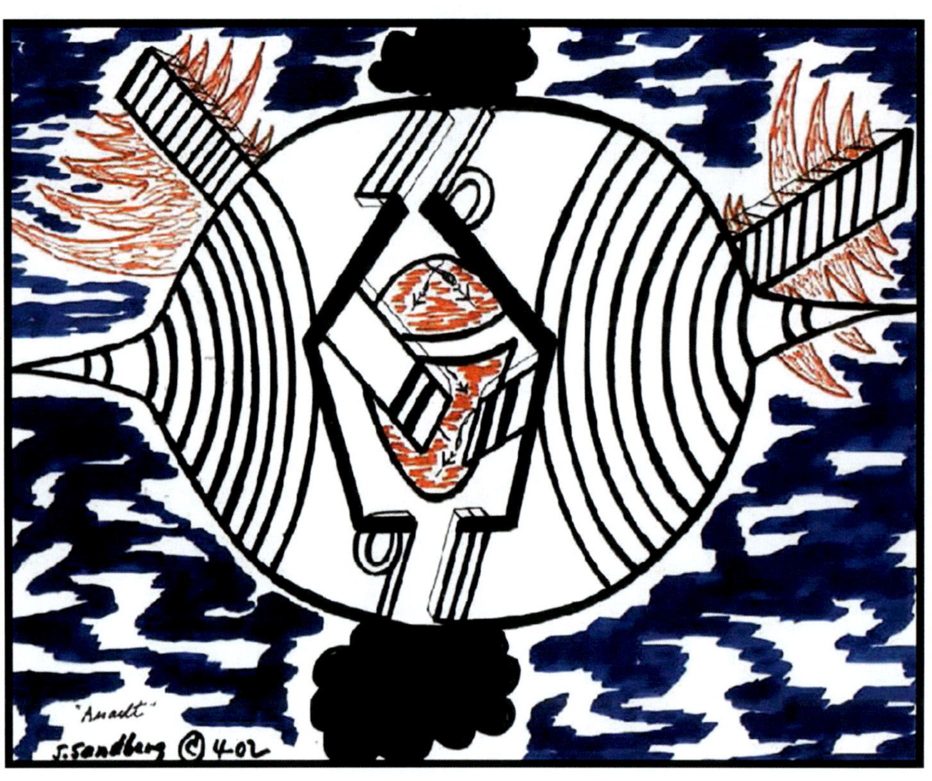

Assault

Enemies' offensive thrust yields devastation from Washington to New York.

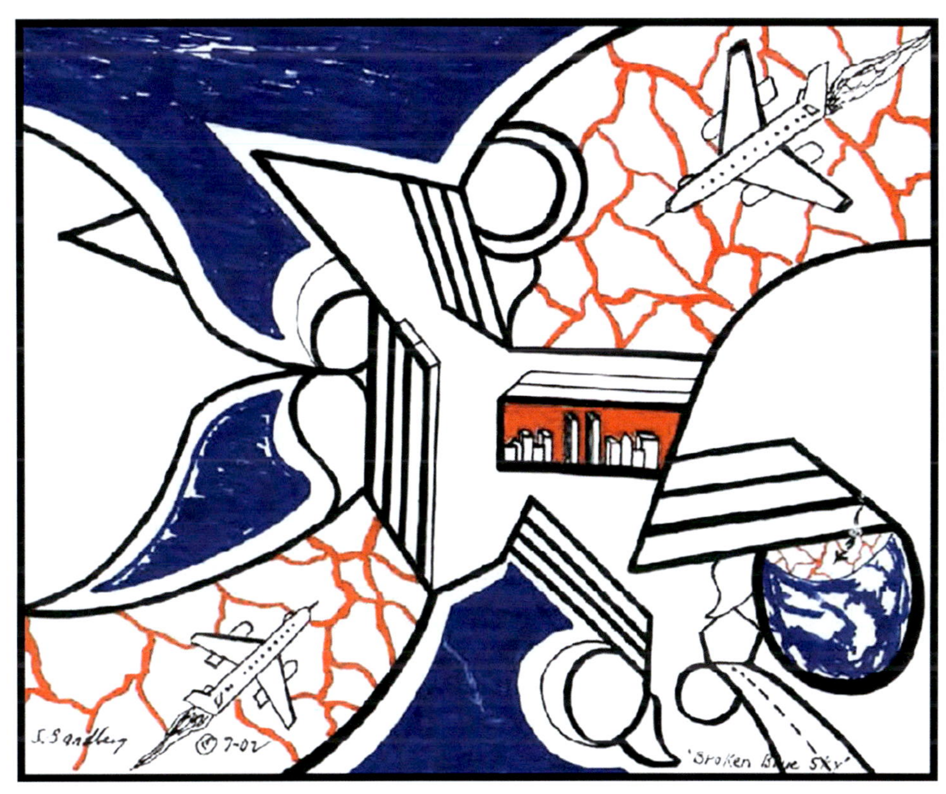

Broken Blue Sky

A stunning beautiful blue sky is soon ruptured.

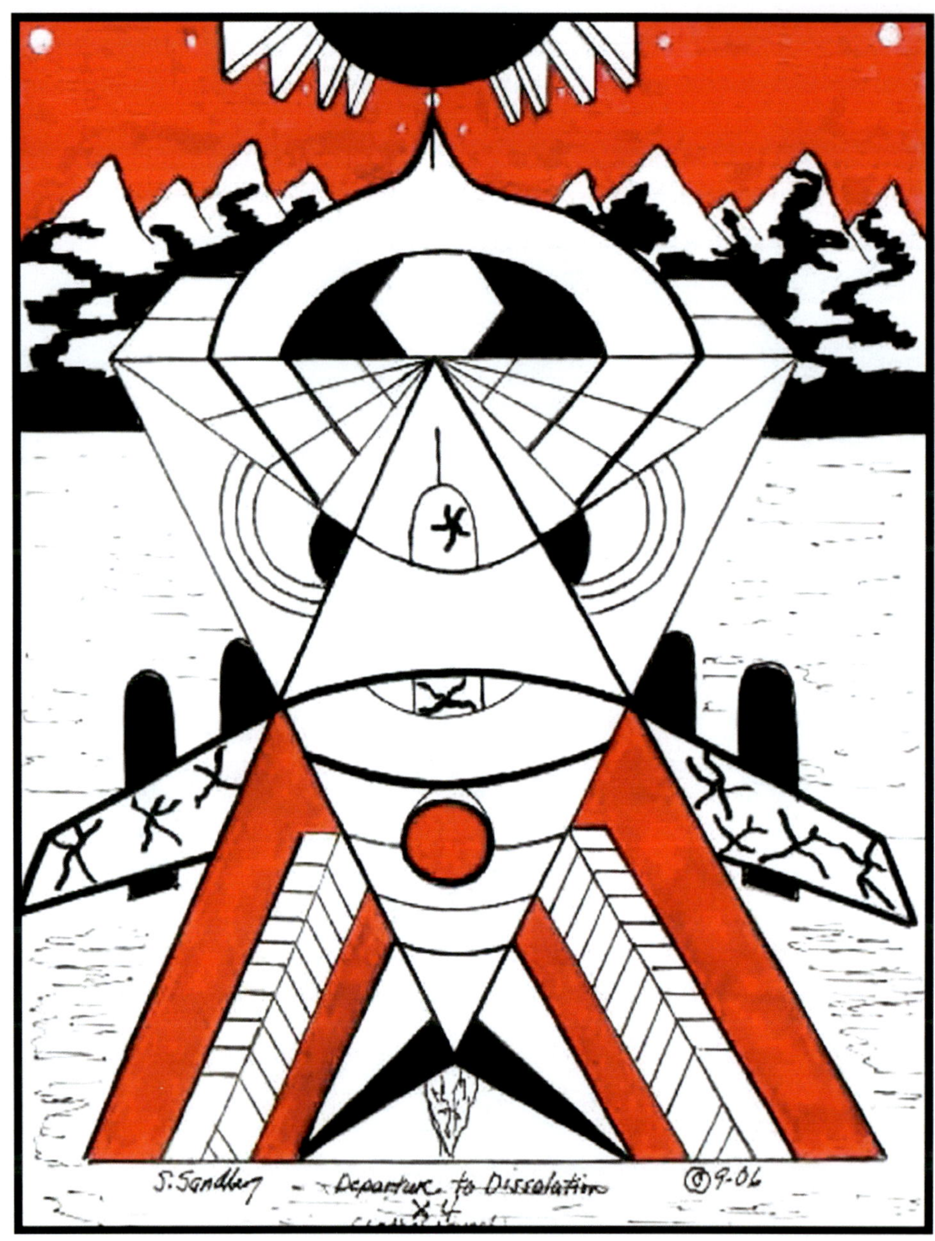

Departure to Dissolution

On that day, there would be no gate arrivals for four planes.

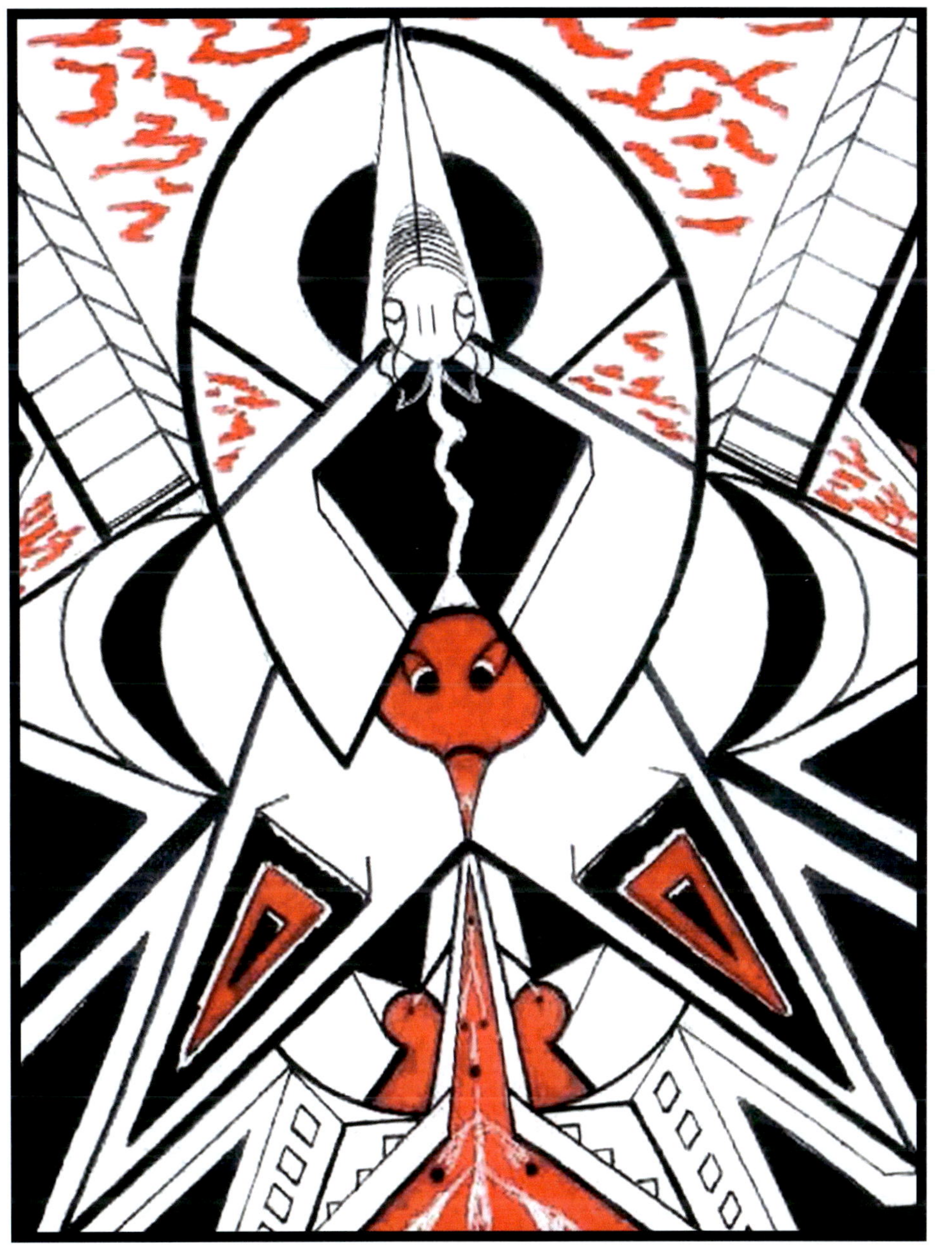

Sinister Symmetries

From the view of the terrorists, the attacks would be well planned
and balanced.

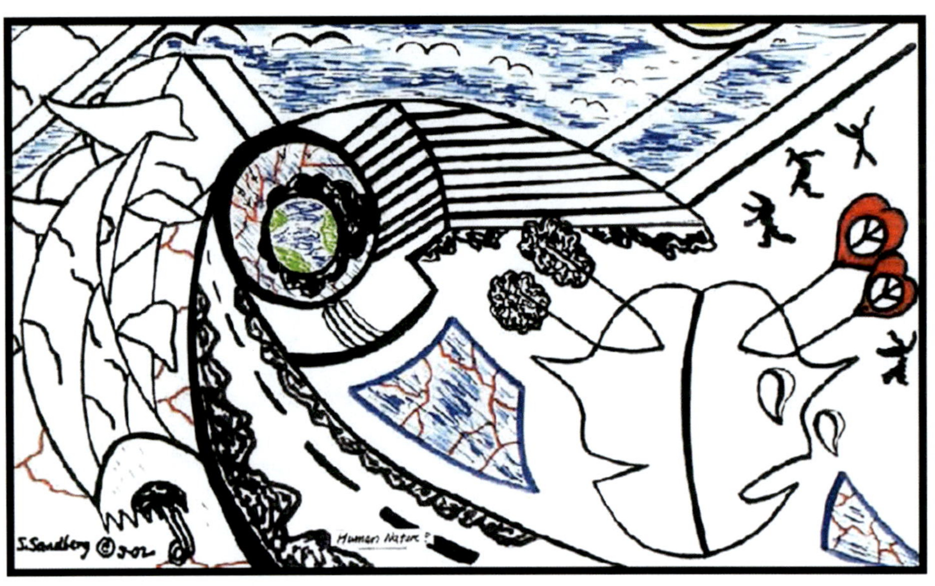

Human Nature?

Mankind's history has always been a struggle between polarizing instincts of good and evil.

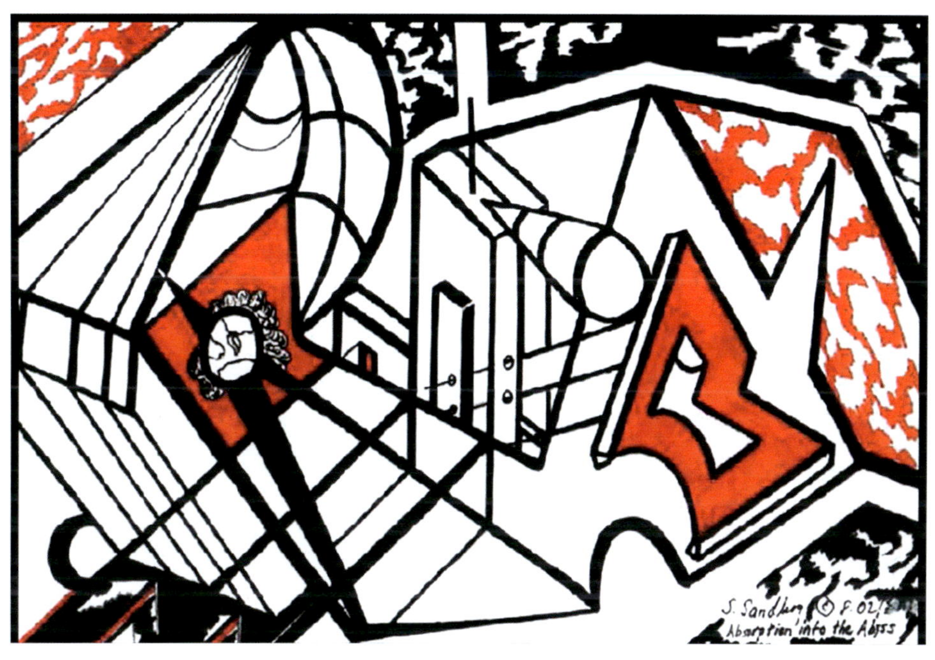

Absorption into the Abyss

Sometimes, the concrete can lead into the abstract. Remnants of reality, though distant, remain.

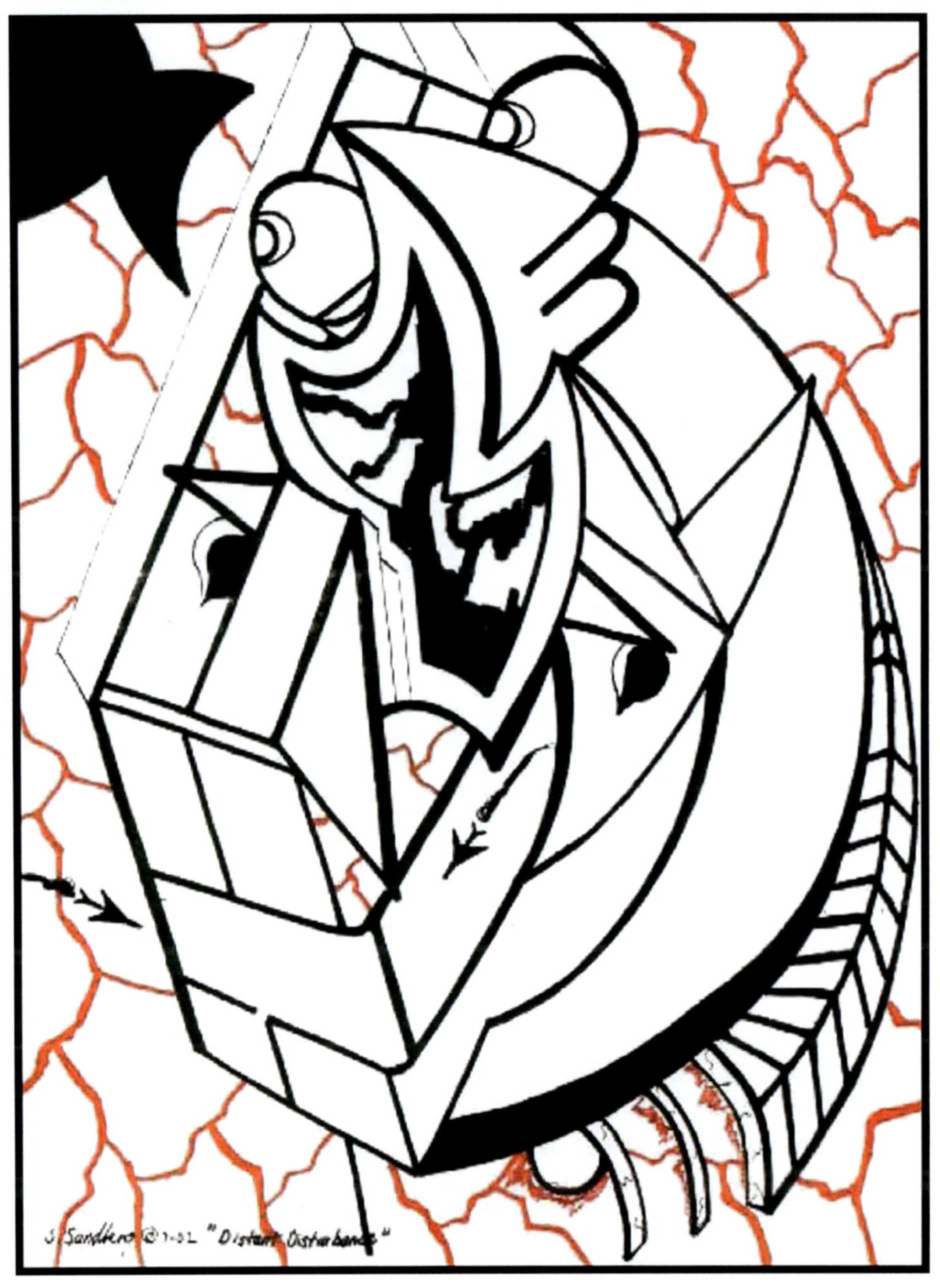

Distant Disturbance

A ripple in the space-time continuum had occurred.

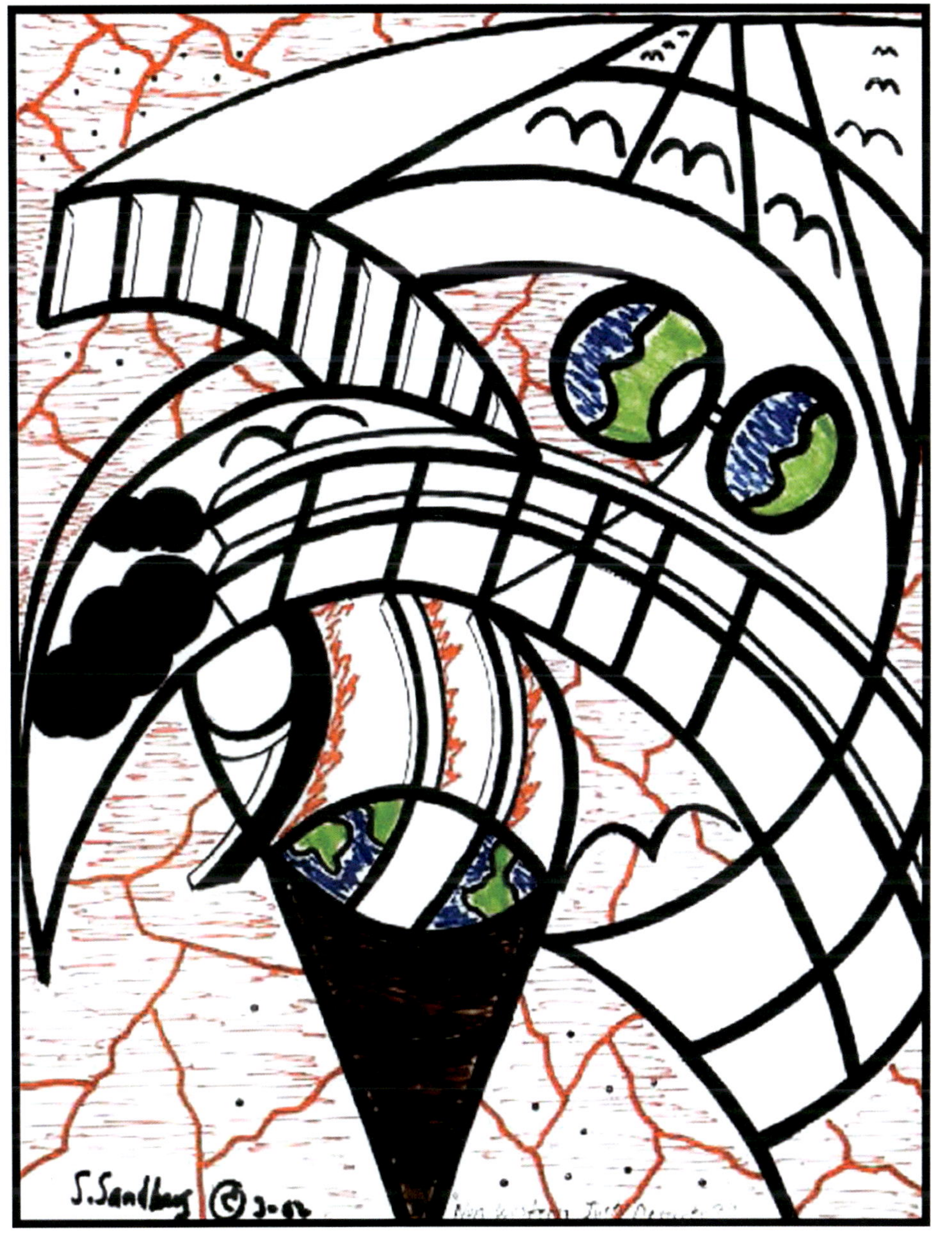

Non-Western Just Desserts?

Extremists from abroad had much on 'their plate' – they hoped
to top it off with something 'sweet'.

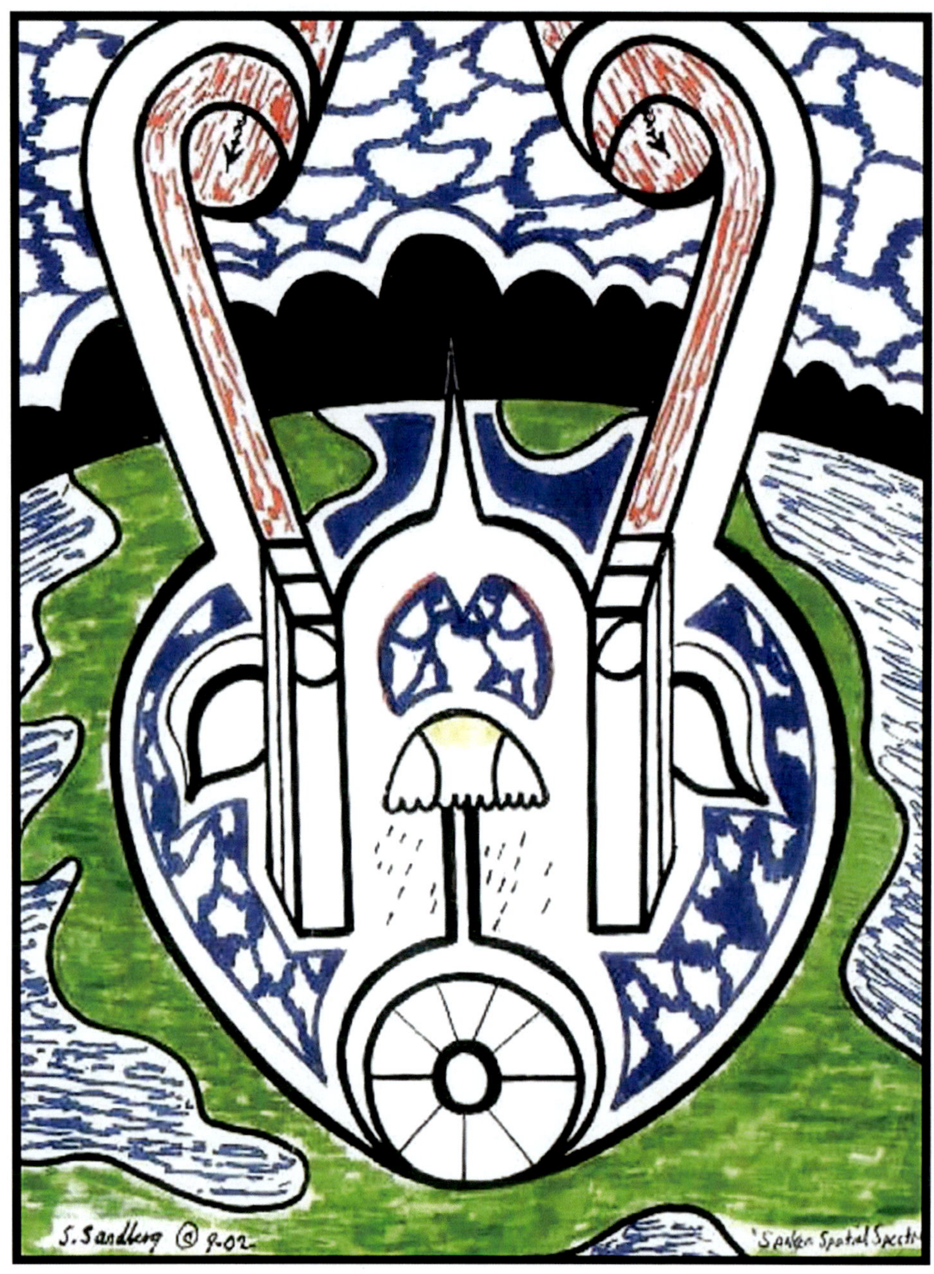

Spoken Spatial Specter

Silence would not be the response from this wounded nation.

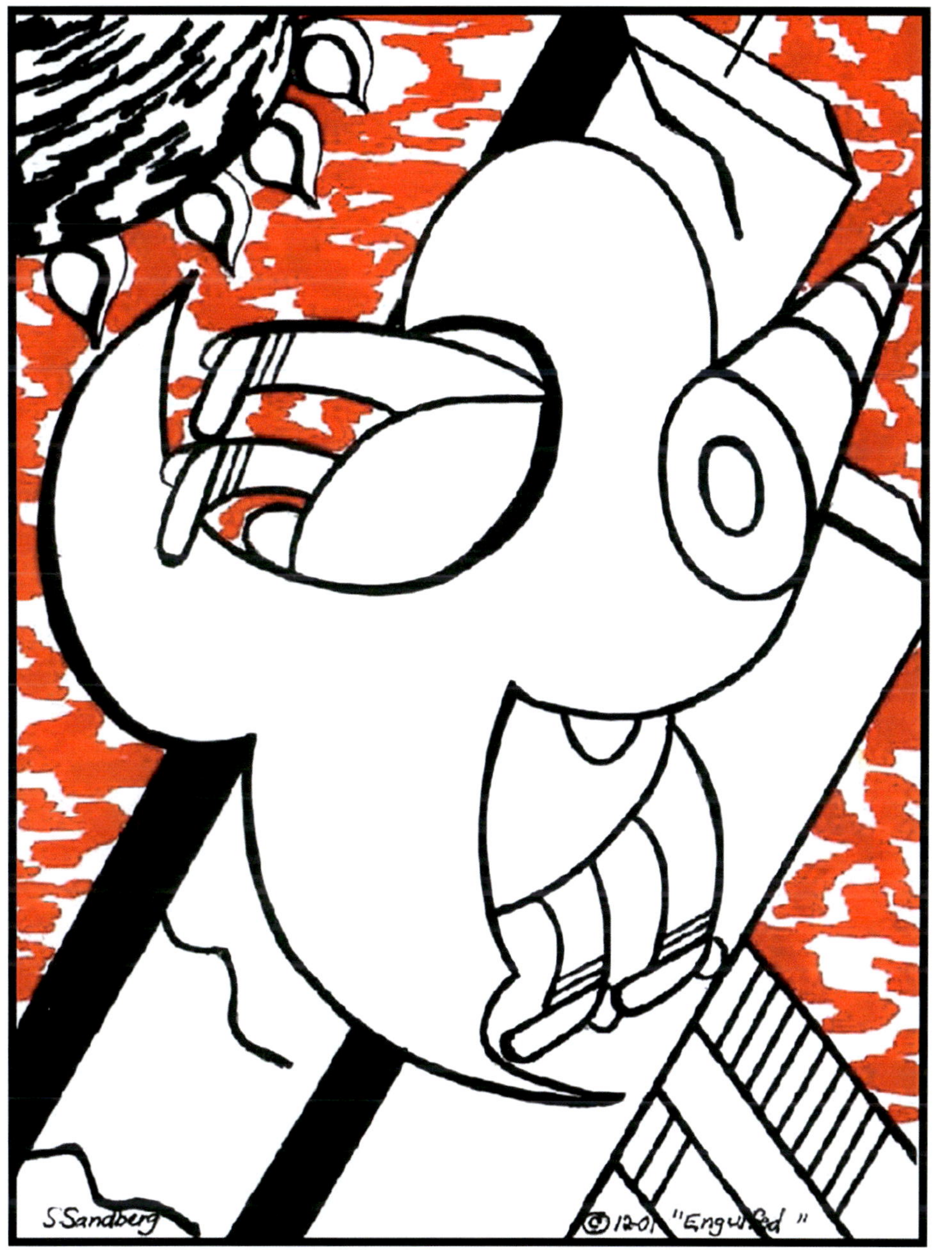

Engulfed

At the time, being consumed in such manner had never seemed possible.

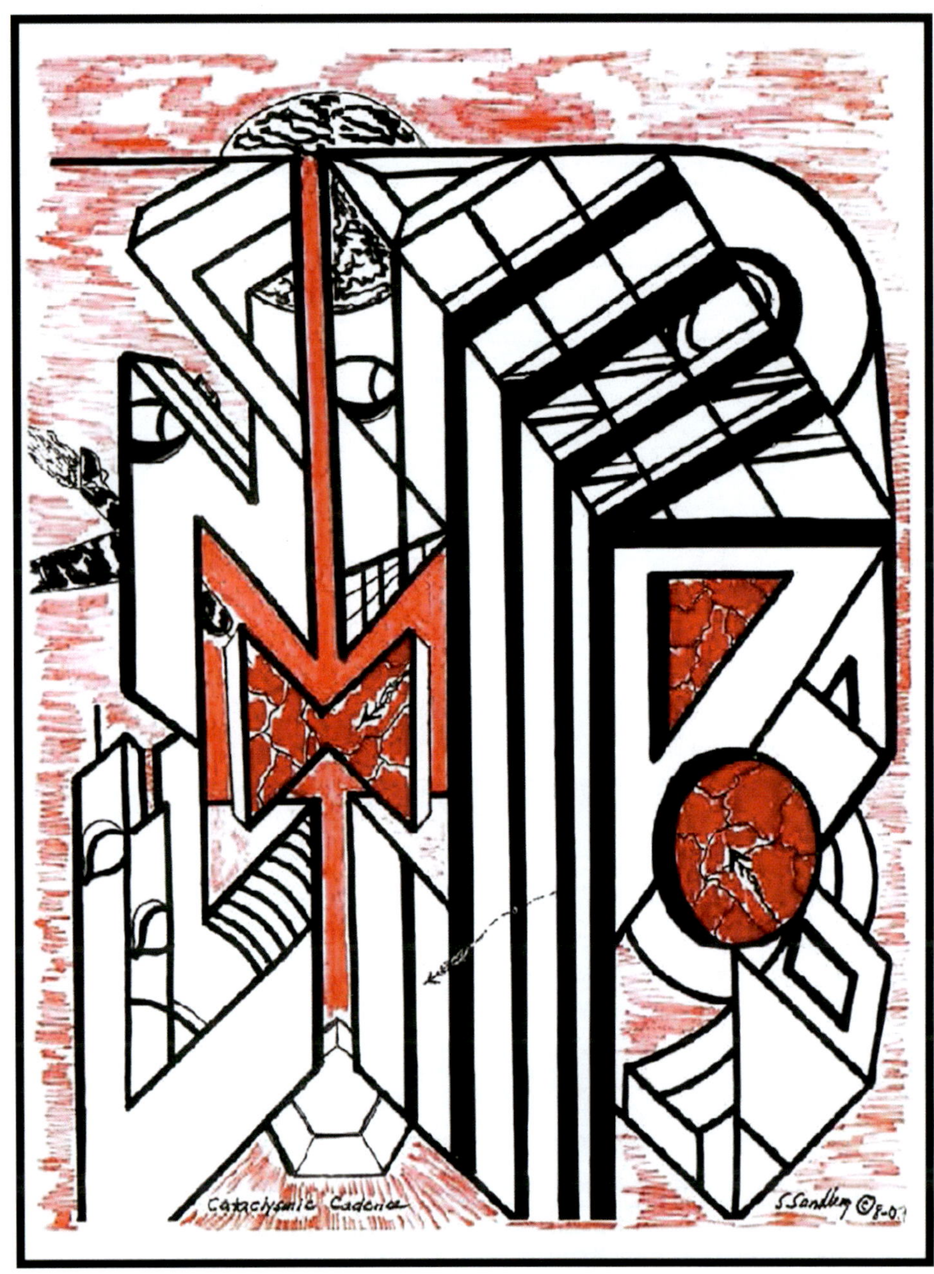

Cataclysmic Cadence

The normal flow of events on a Tuesday morning
changed abruptly.

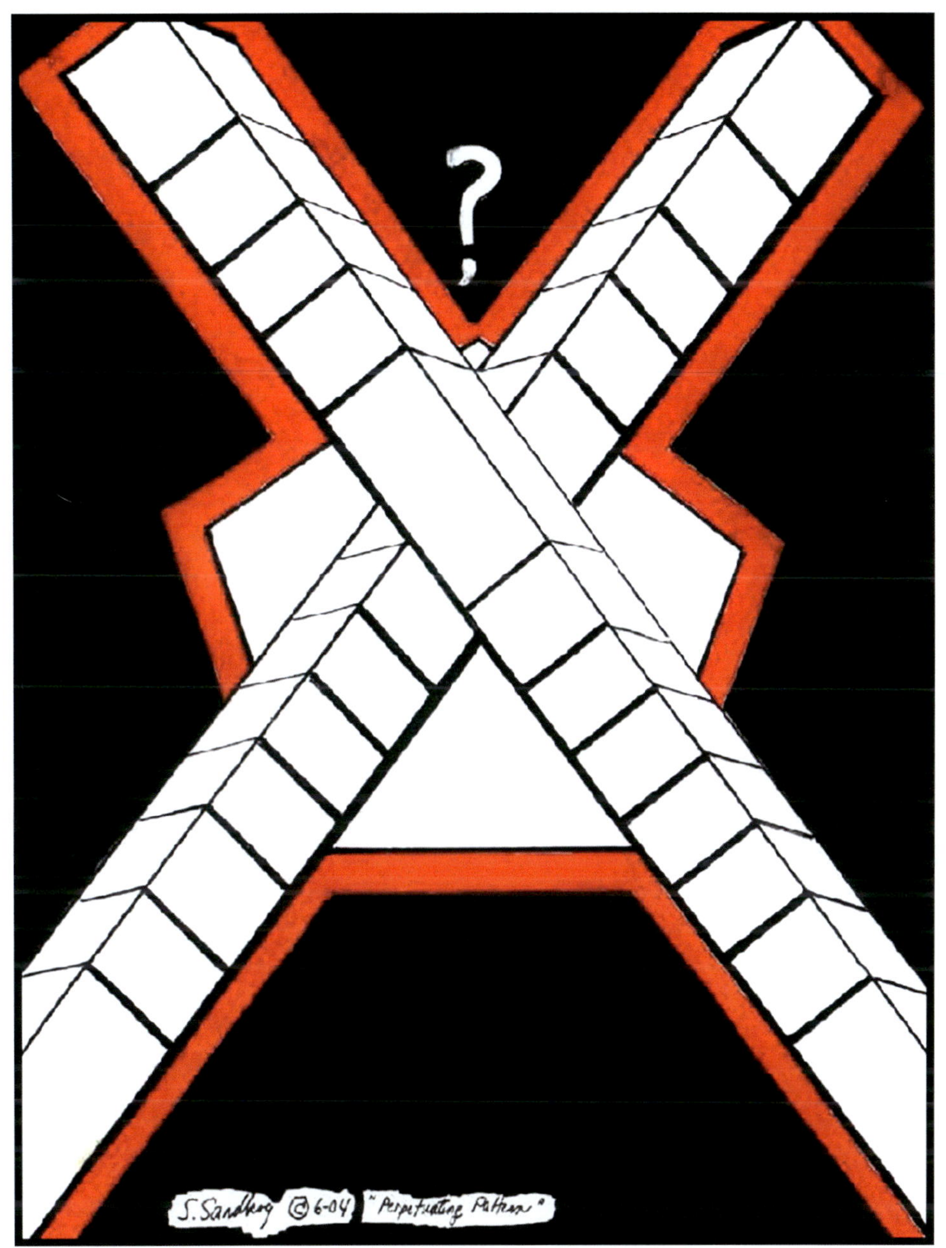

Perpetuating Pattern

The haunting visual continues to resonate.

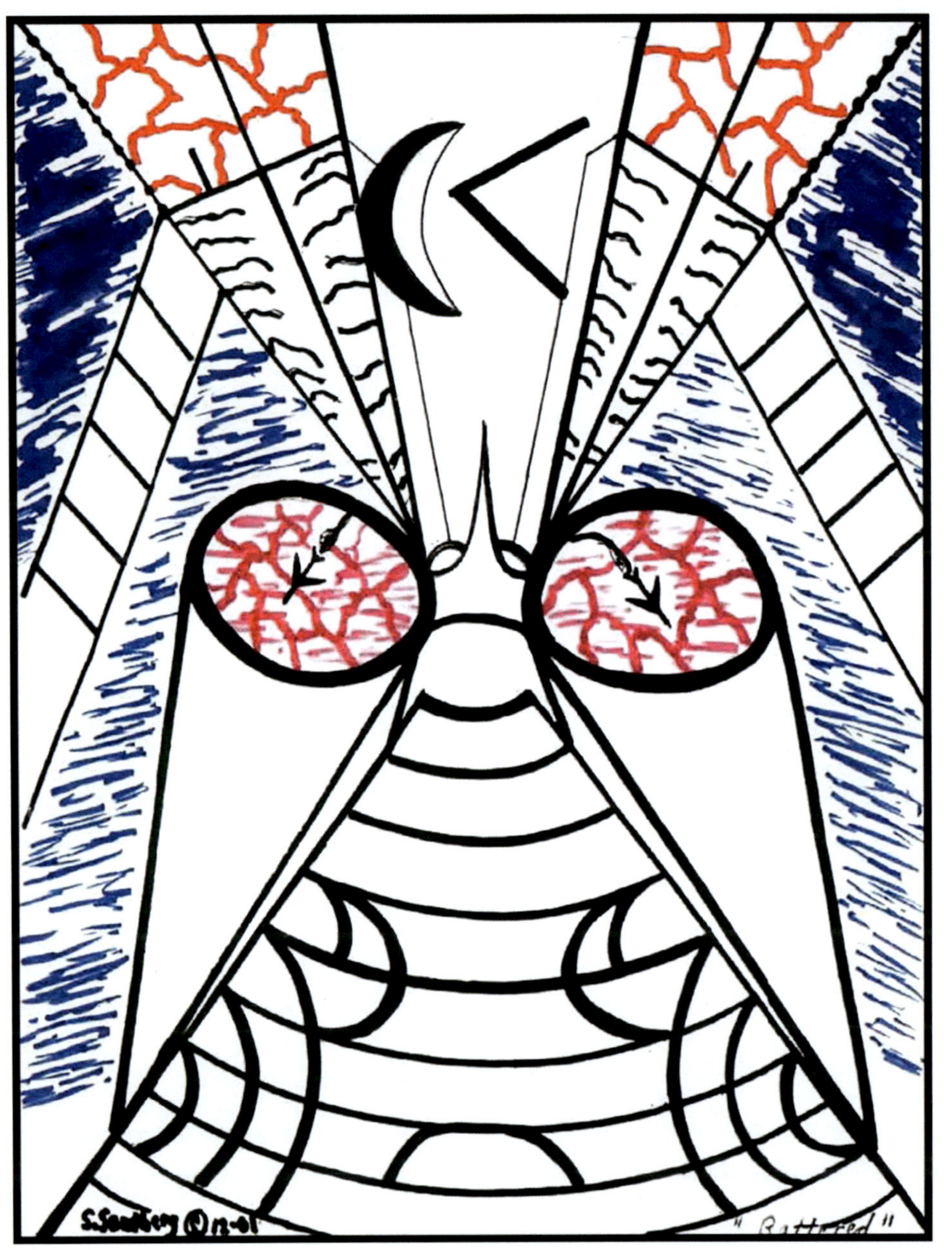

Battered

Early 21st century dawn has sun set on thousands.

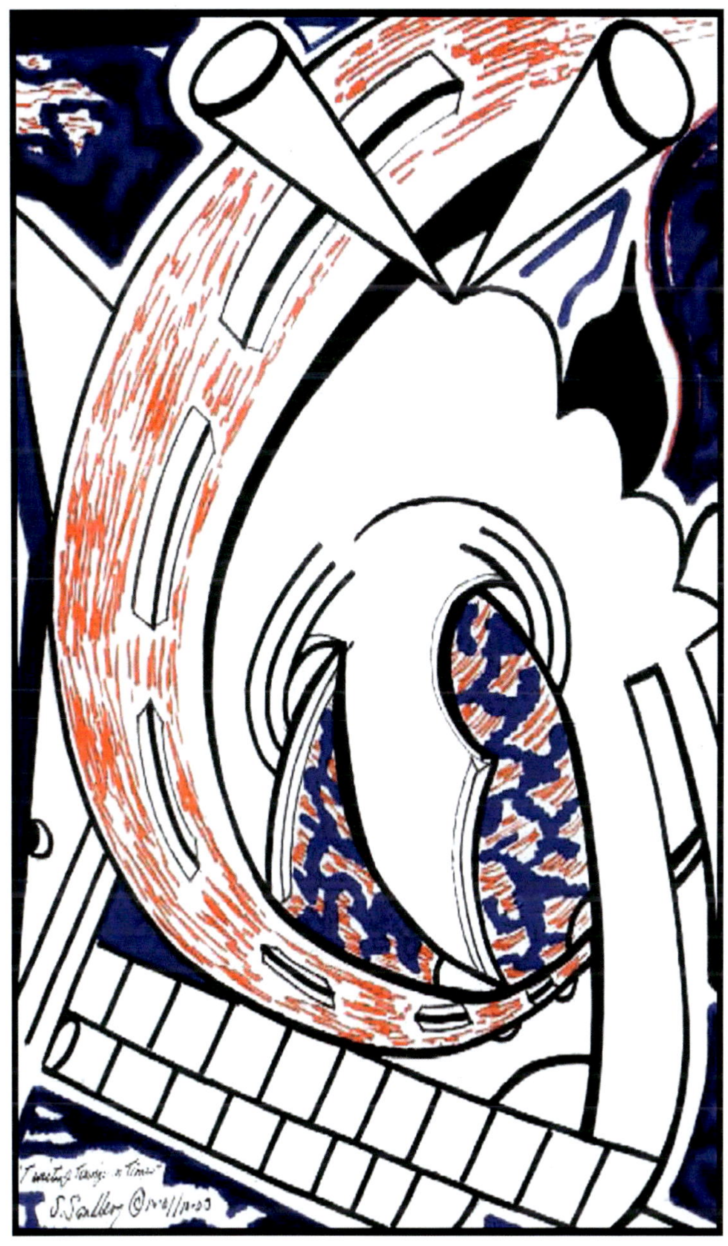

Twisting Twinge in Time

Major disruptions in time occur that affect views of the past and charting the future.

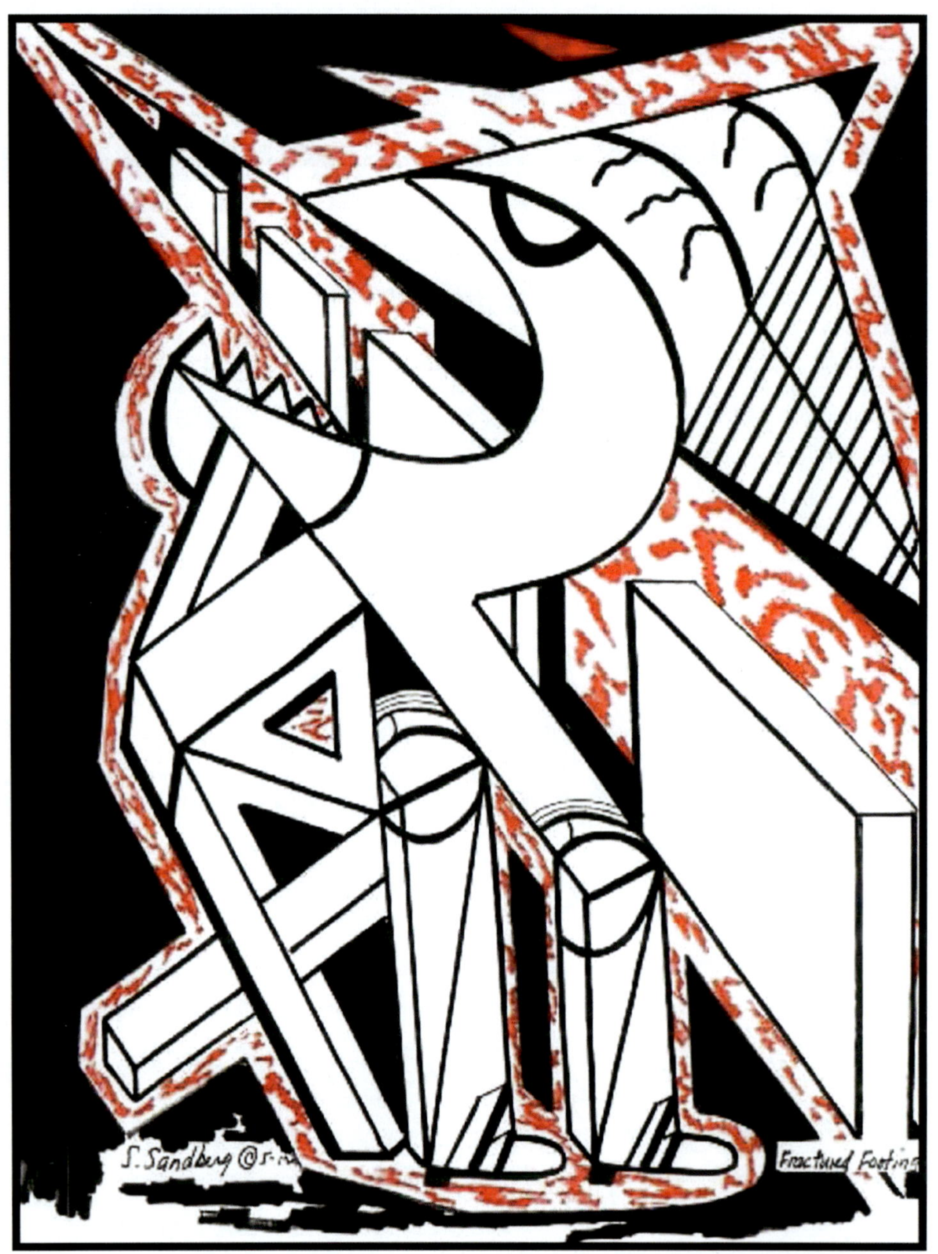

Fractured Footing

Unquestionable belief in the certainty of homeland
security would never again be possible.

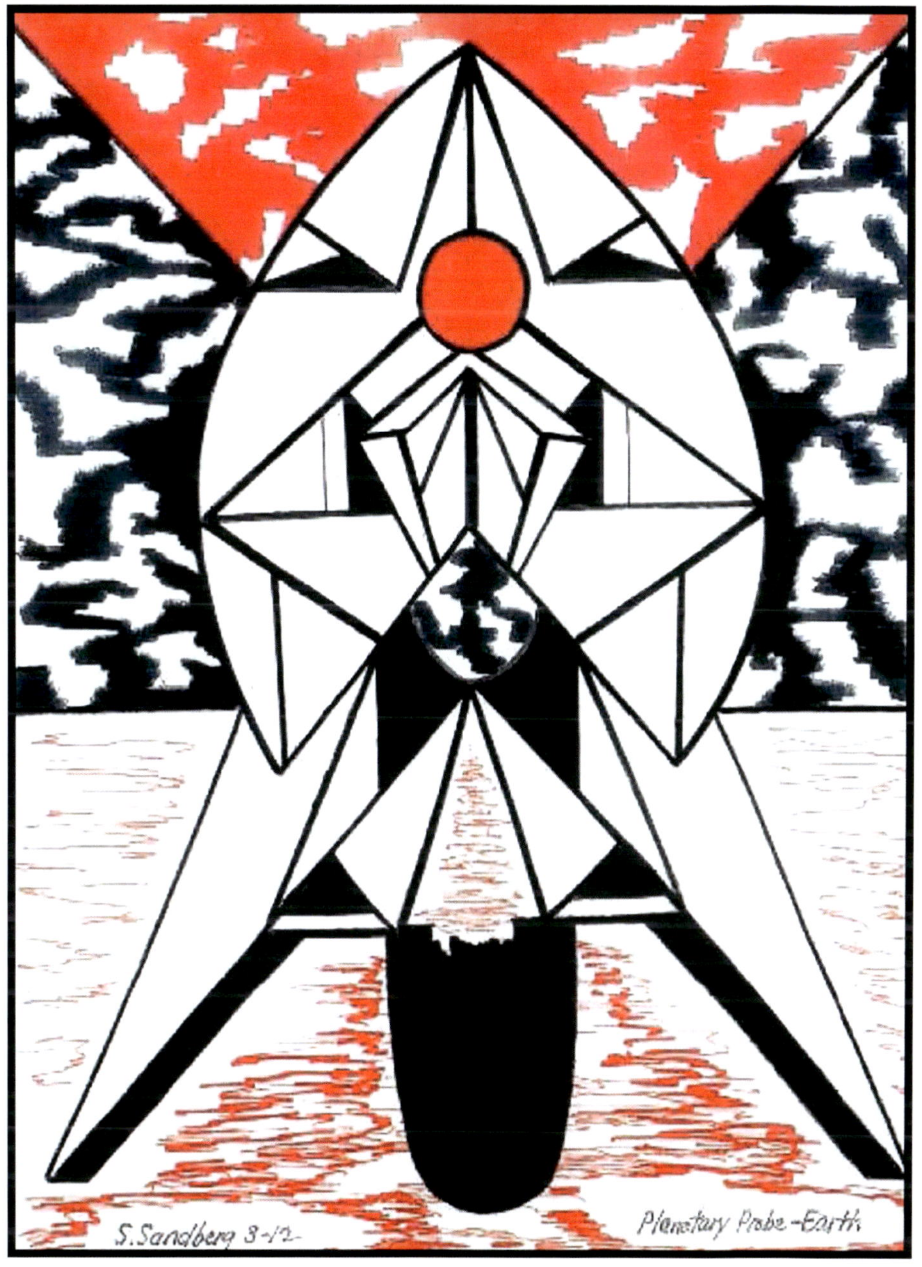

Planetary Probe-Earth

A future extraterrestrial discovery reveals the sad truth that once thriving civilizations held dominion on a now barren and sterile world.

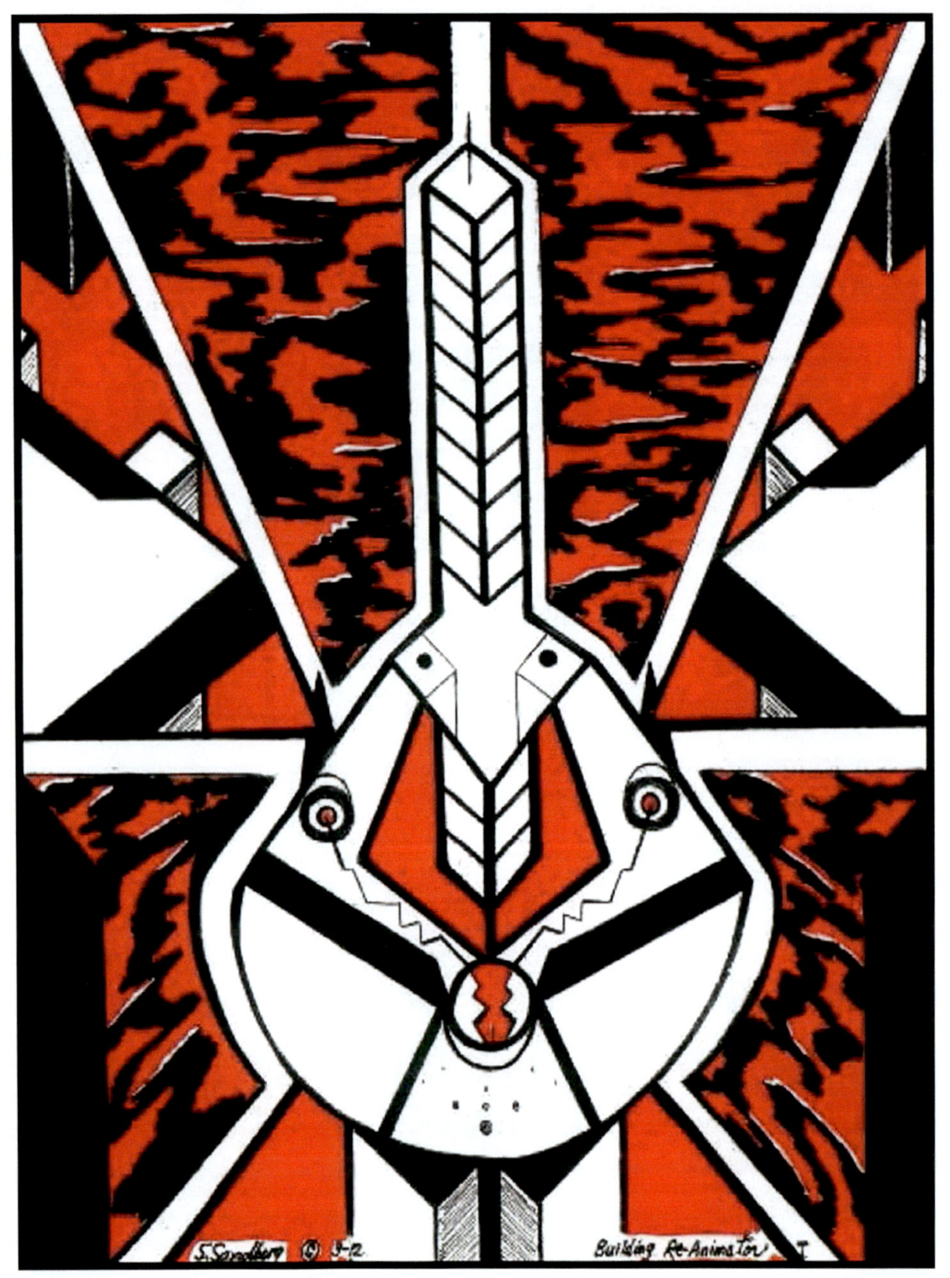

Building Re-Animator I

In the world of fantasy, everything is possible and…

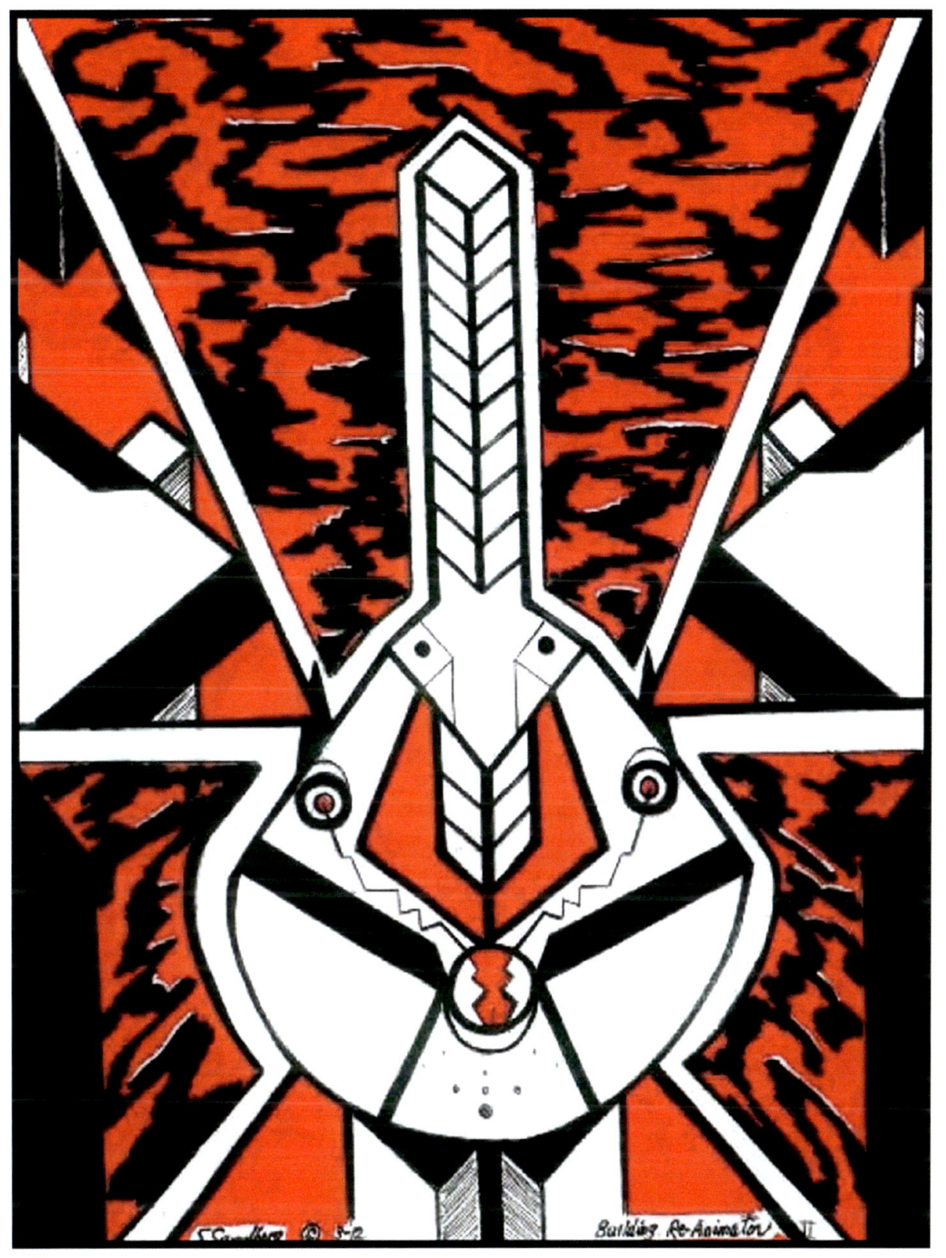

Building Re-Animator II

An artist's stroke can provide rapid construction out of chaos.

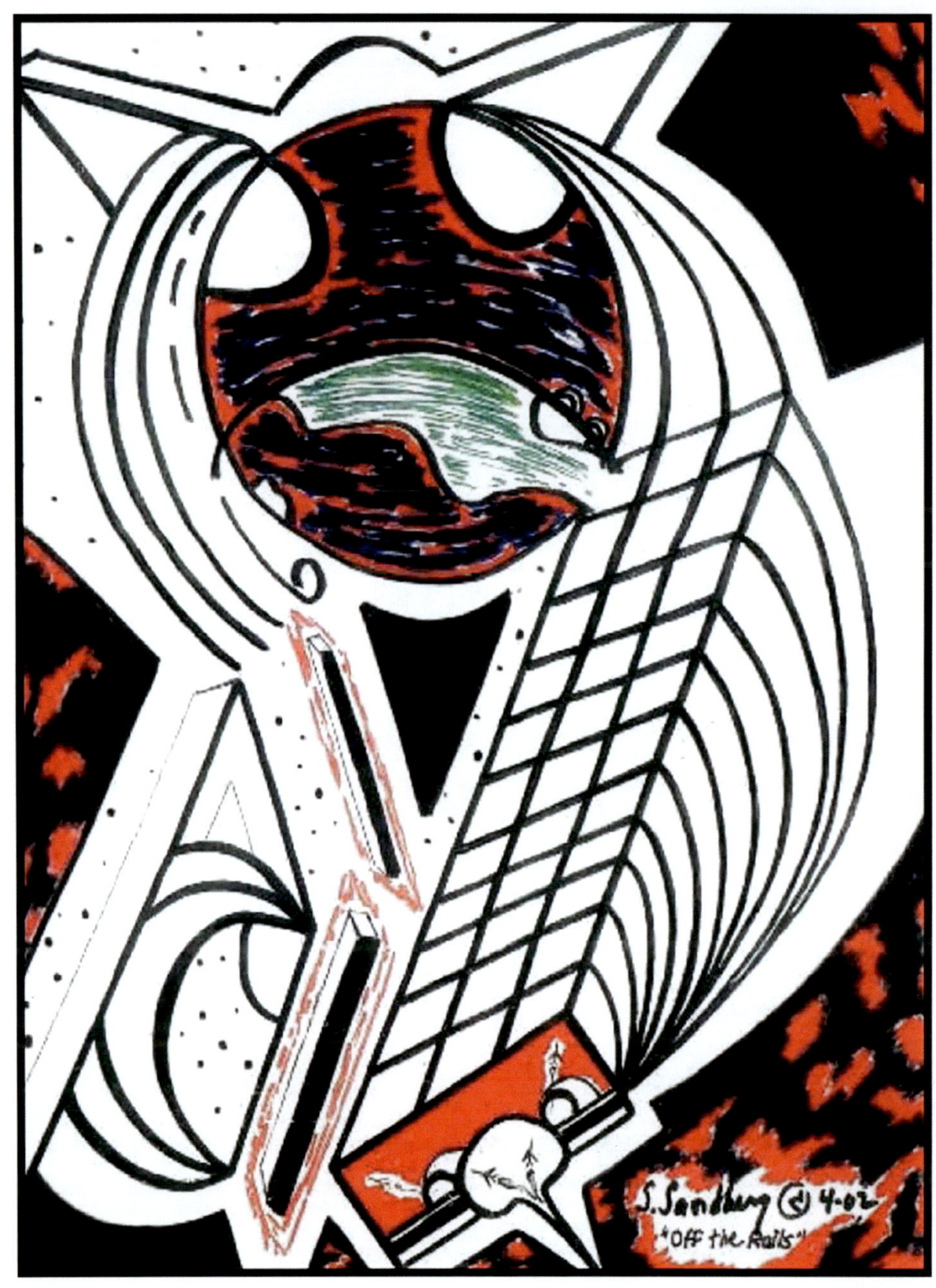

Off the Rails

Many Americans became unhinged as their world appeared to be knocked off its axis.

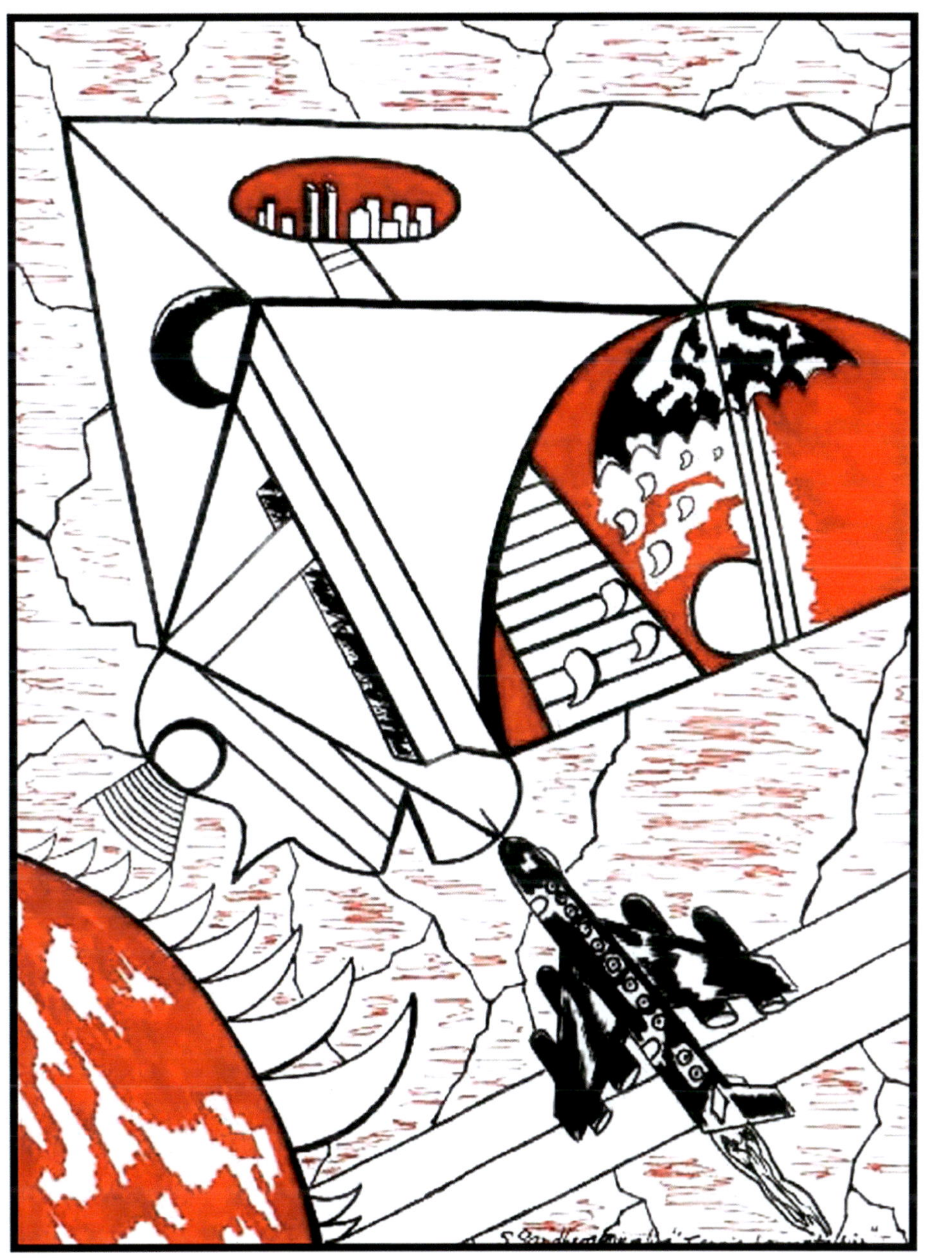

Iconic Lamentation

A picture of grief that still swirls in the mind.

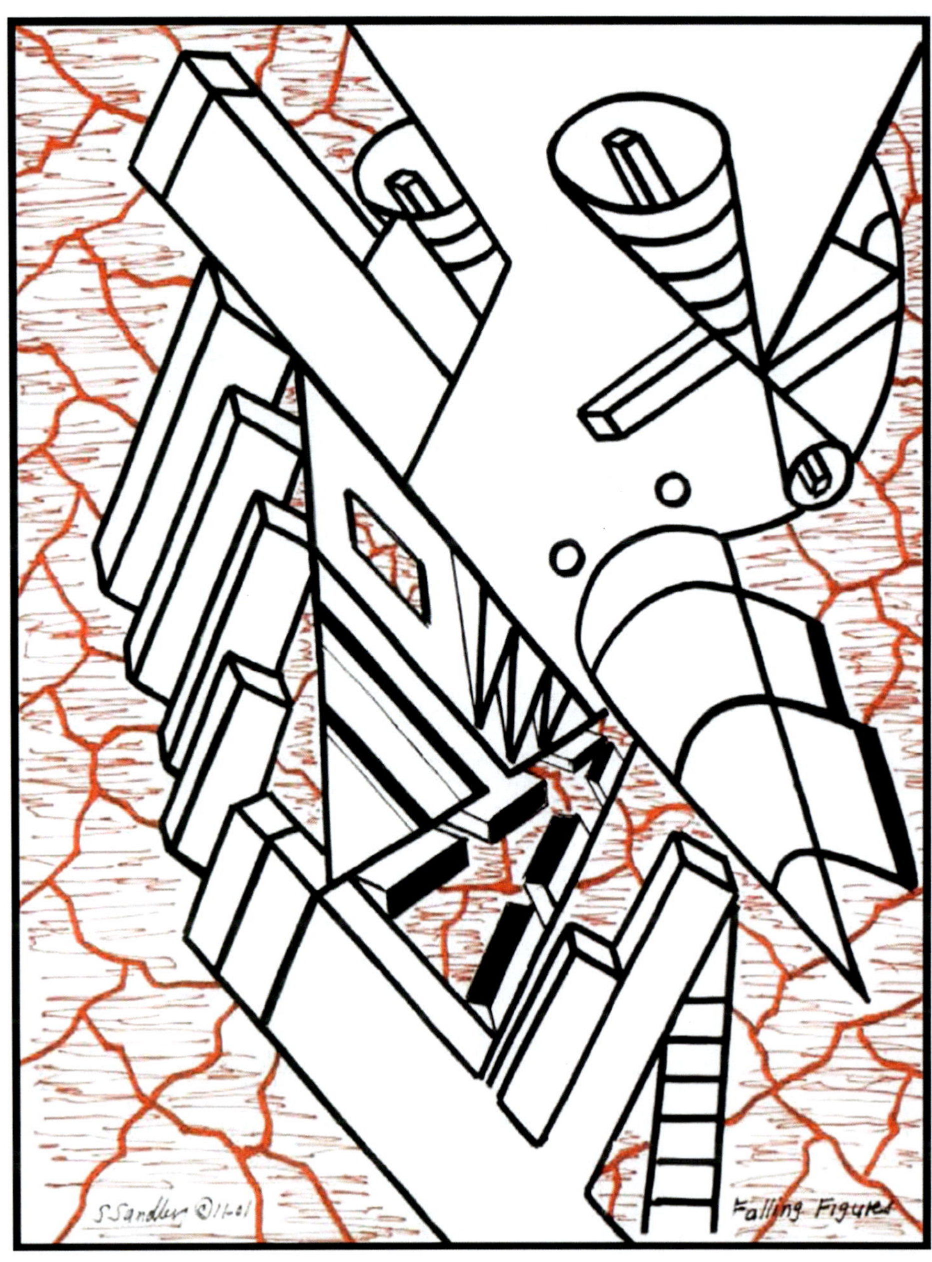

Falling Figures

The structures in our lives had been toppled.

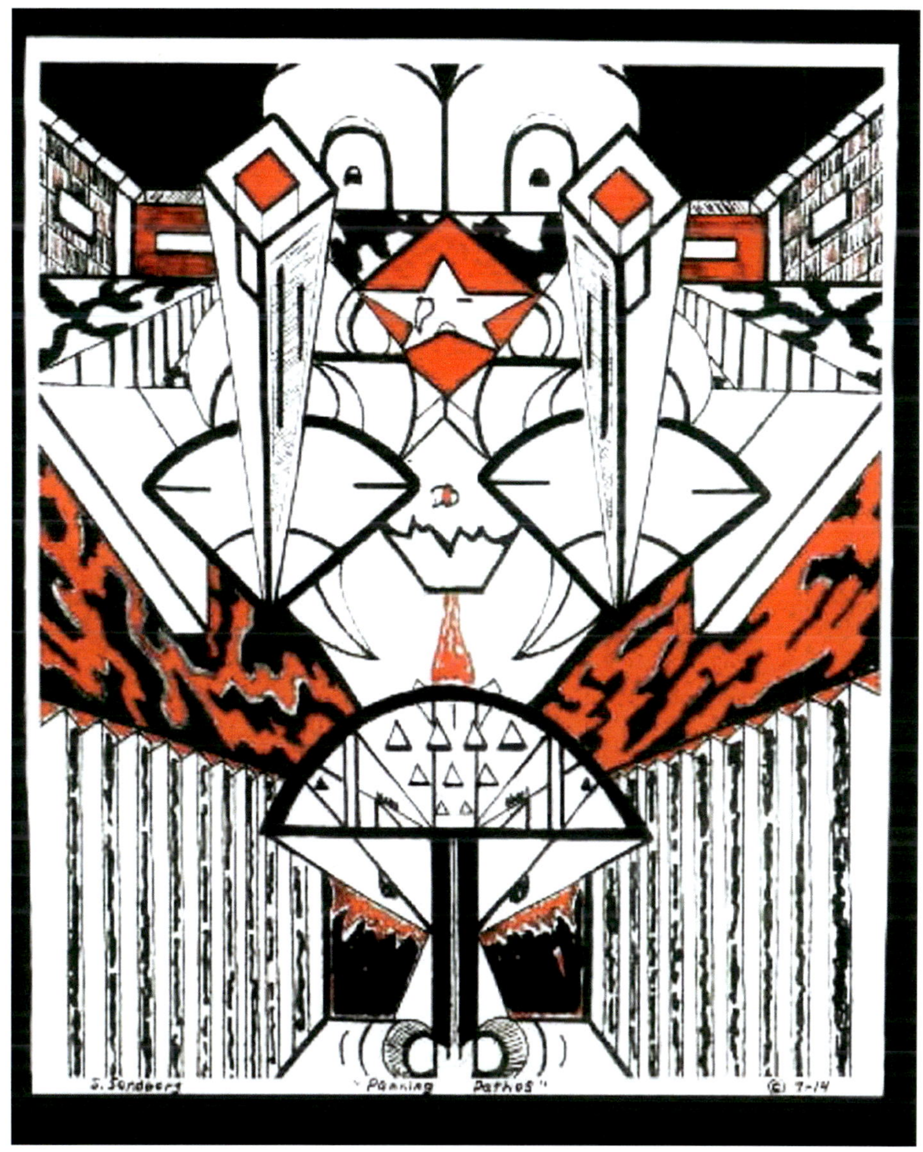

Panning Pathos

With widened optics, one cannot help but see the need
for deep compassion.

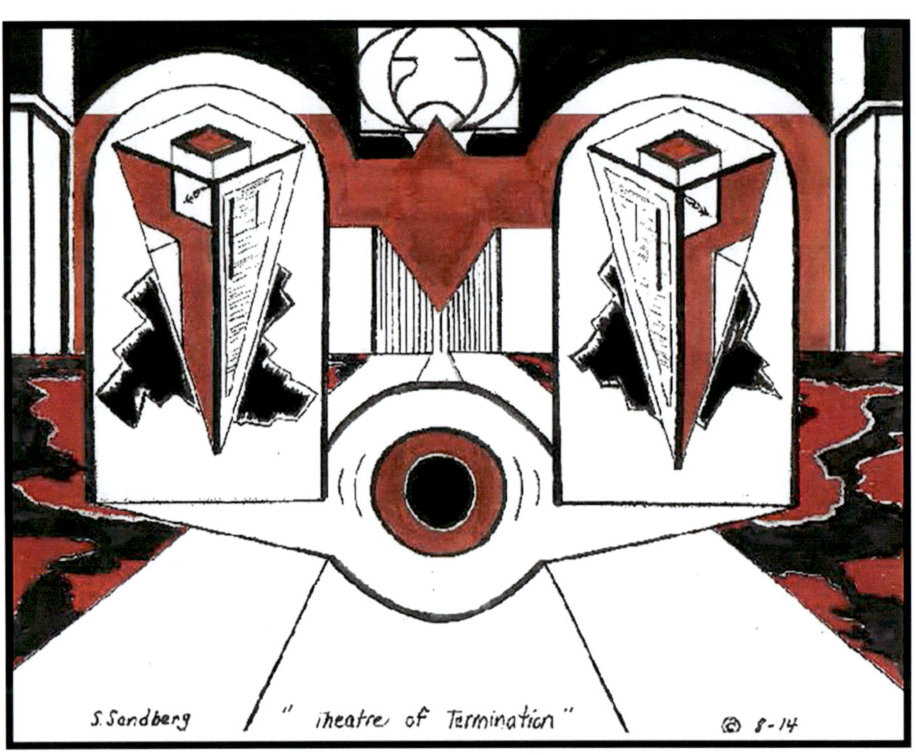

Theatre of Termination

A place where no one could envision that Evil would have taken center stage.

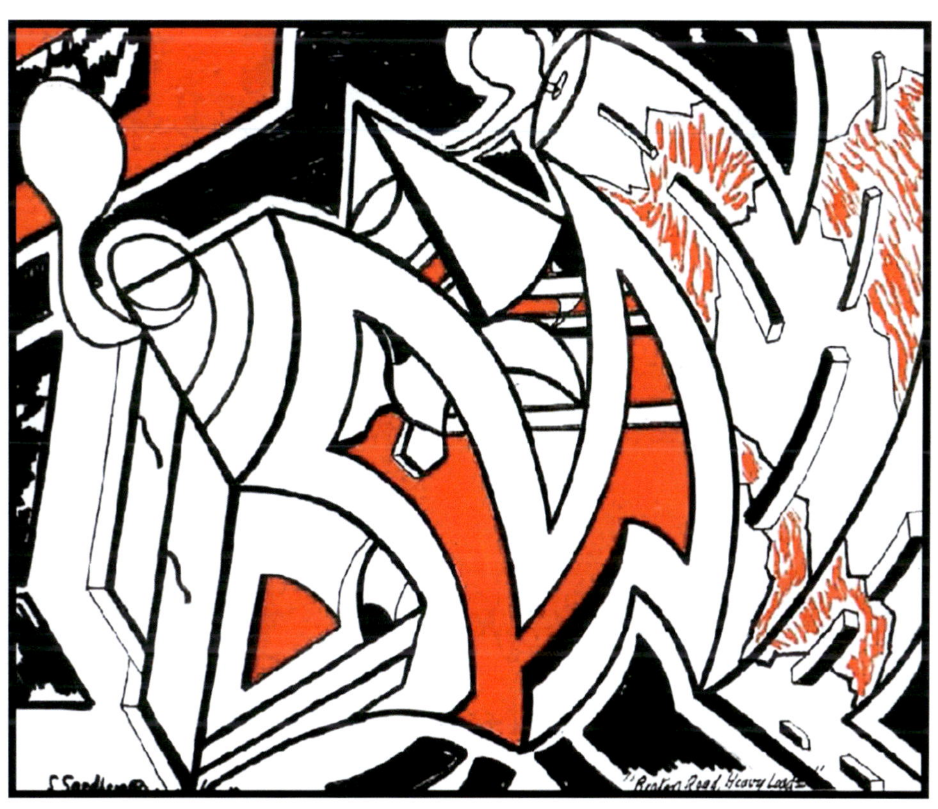

Broken Road, Heavy Load

They didn't have a ghost of a chance!

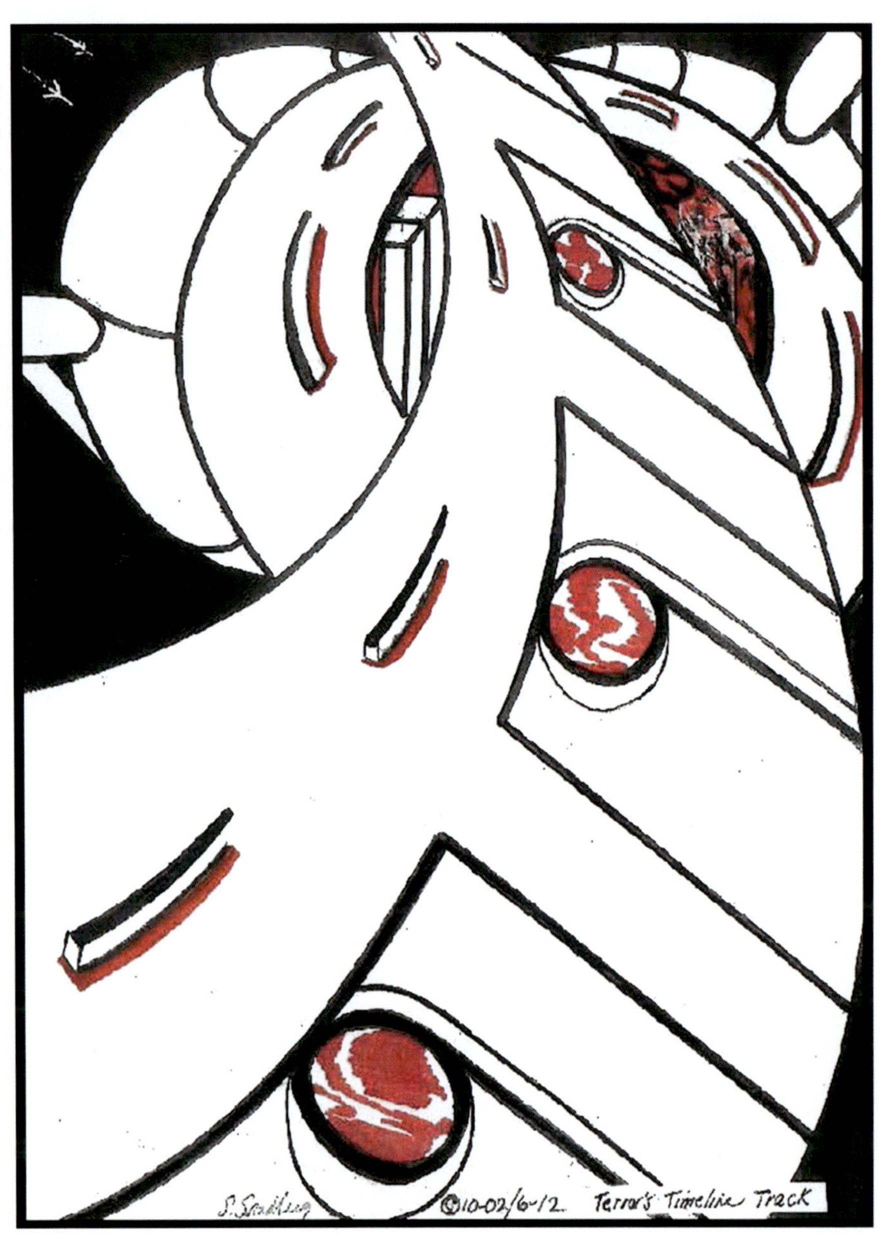

Terror's Timeline Track

A month, a day, a disaster!

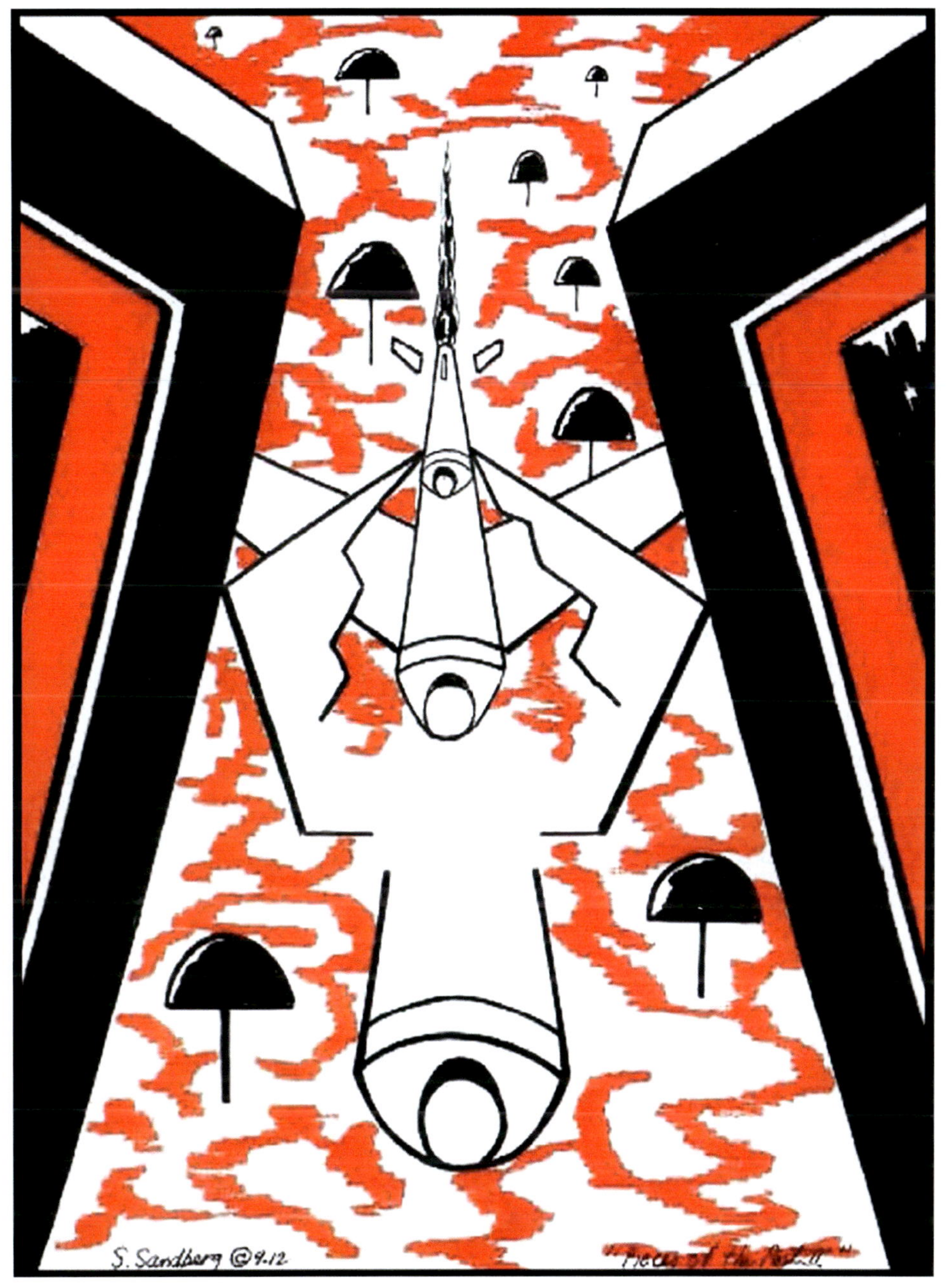

Pieces of the Past

Memories remain as fragments, over time they FADE,
Fade, fade, but never quite disappear.

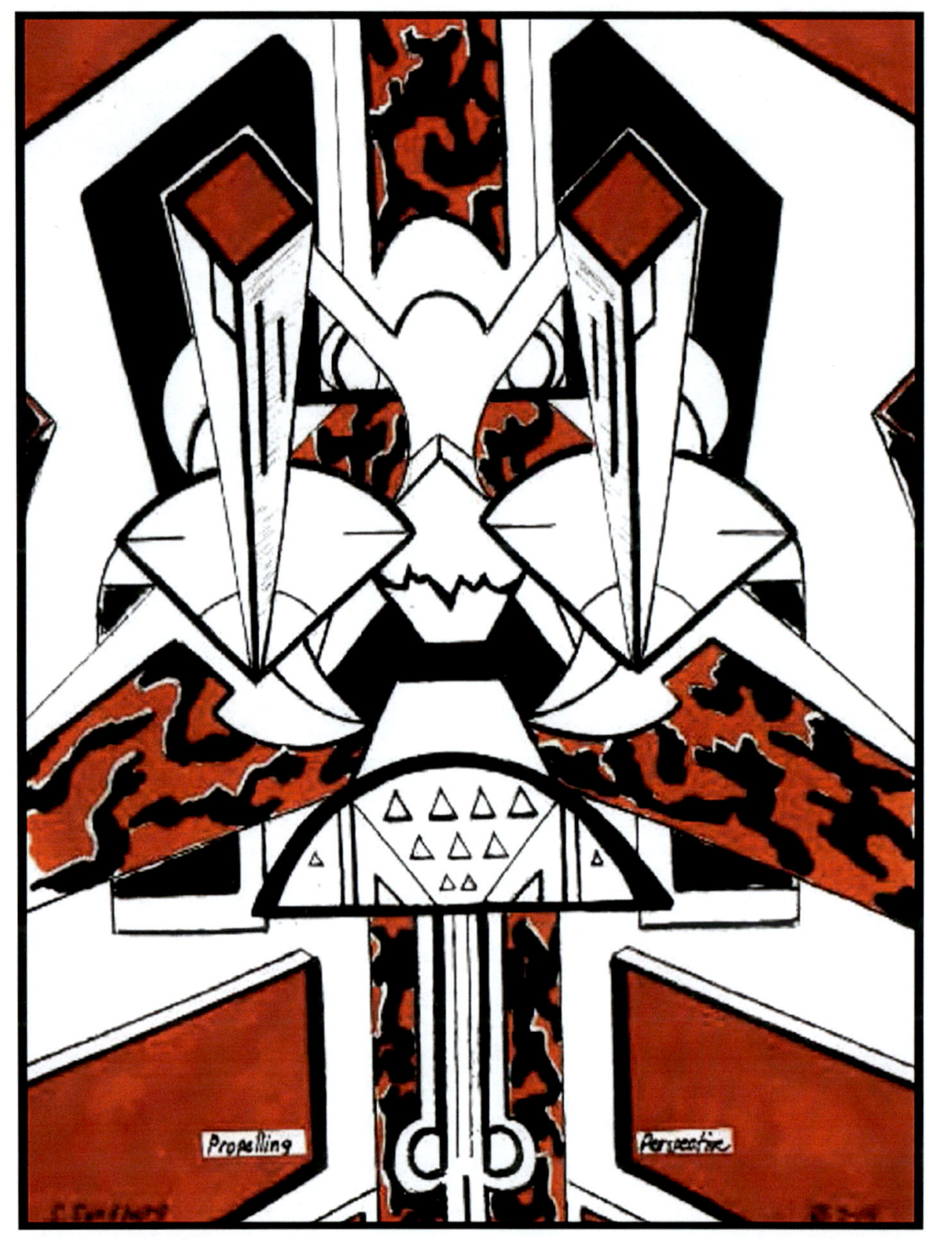

Propelling Perspective

Years later, the driving force as viewed from above,
still remains poignant.

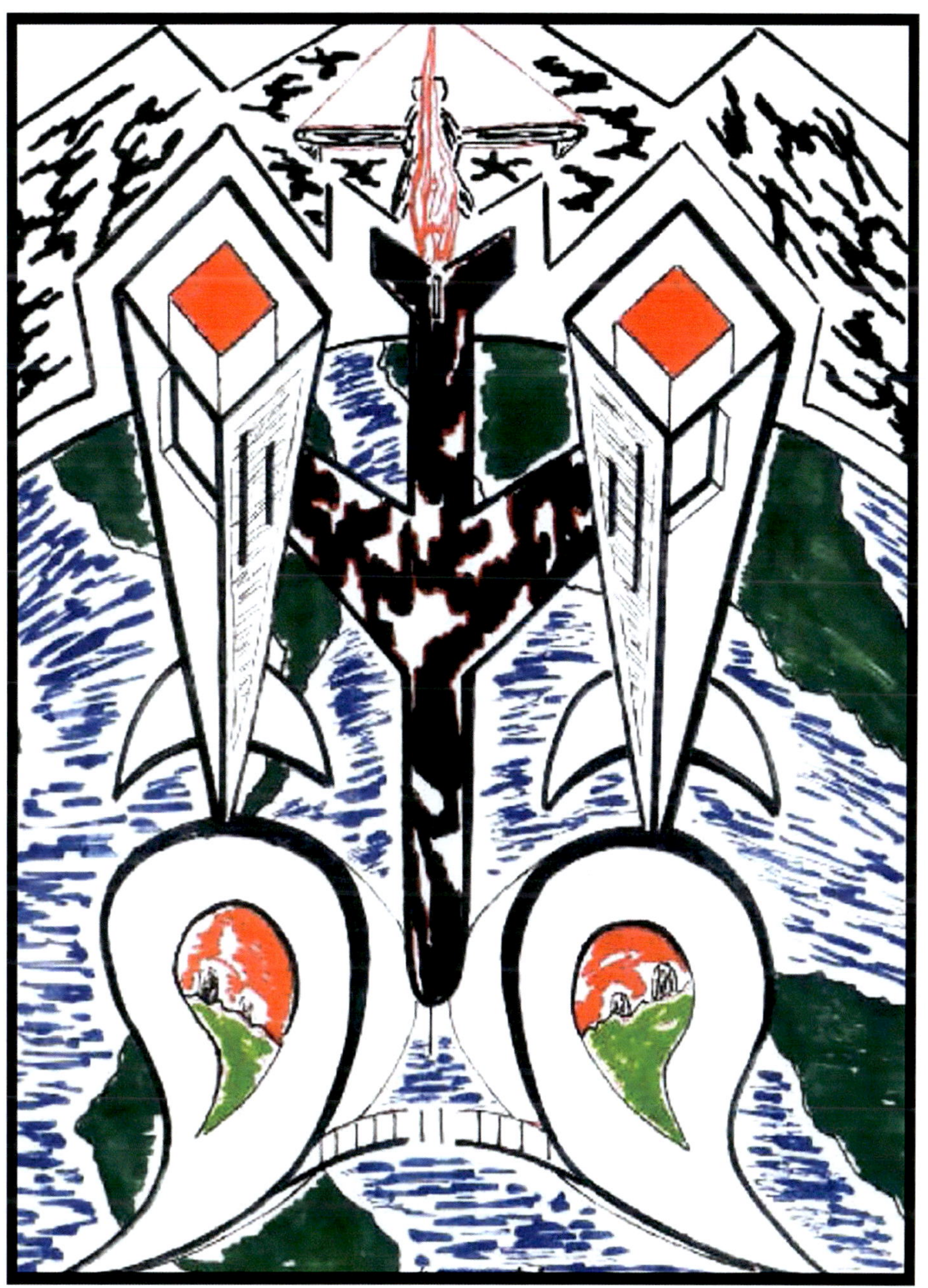

Descent

Is it inevitable that the downward spiral continues?

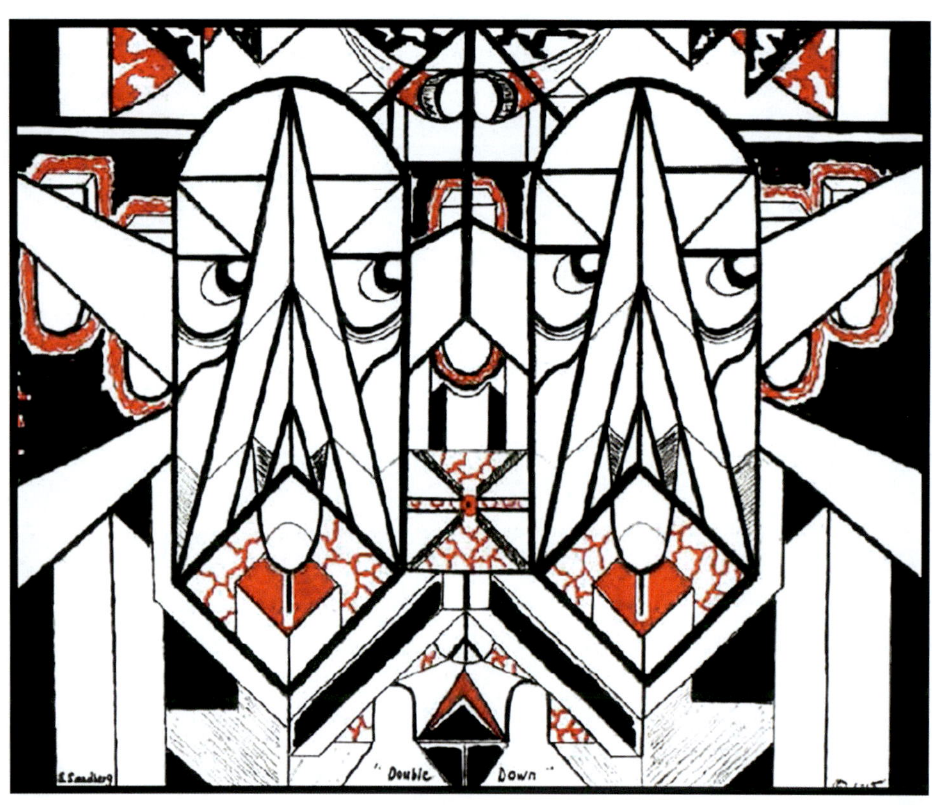

Double Down

They gambled! Ultimately they will LOSE!

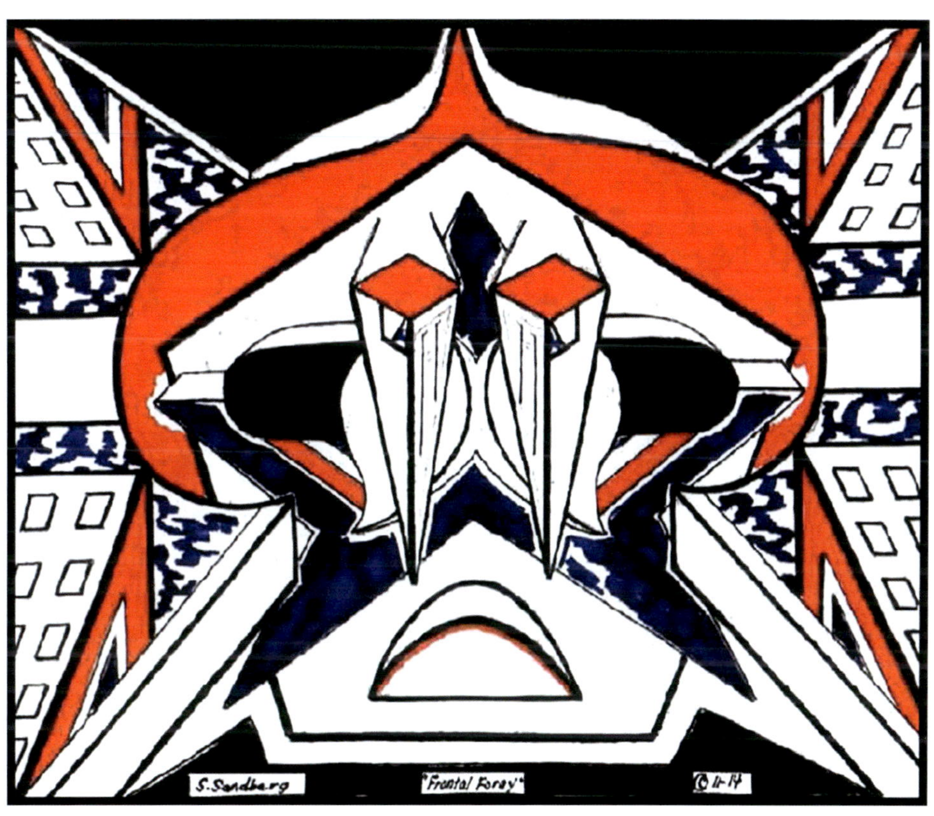

Frontal Foray

It was like a shot in the face.

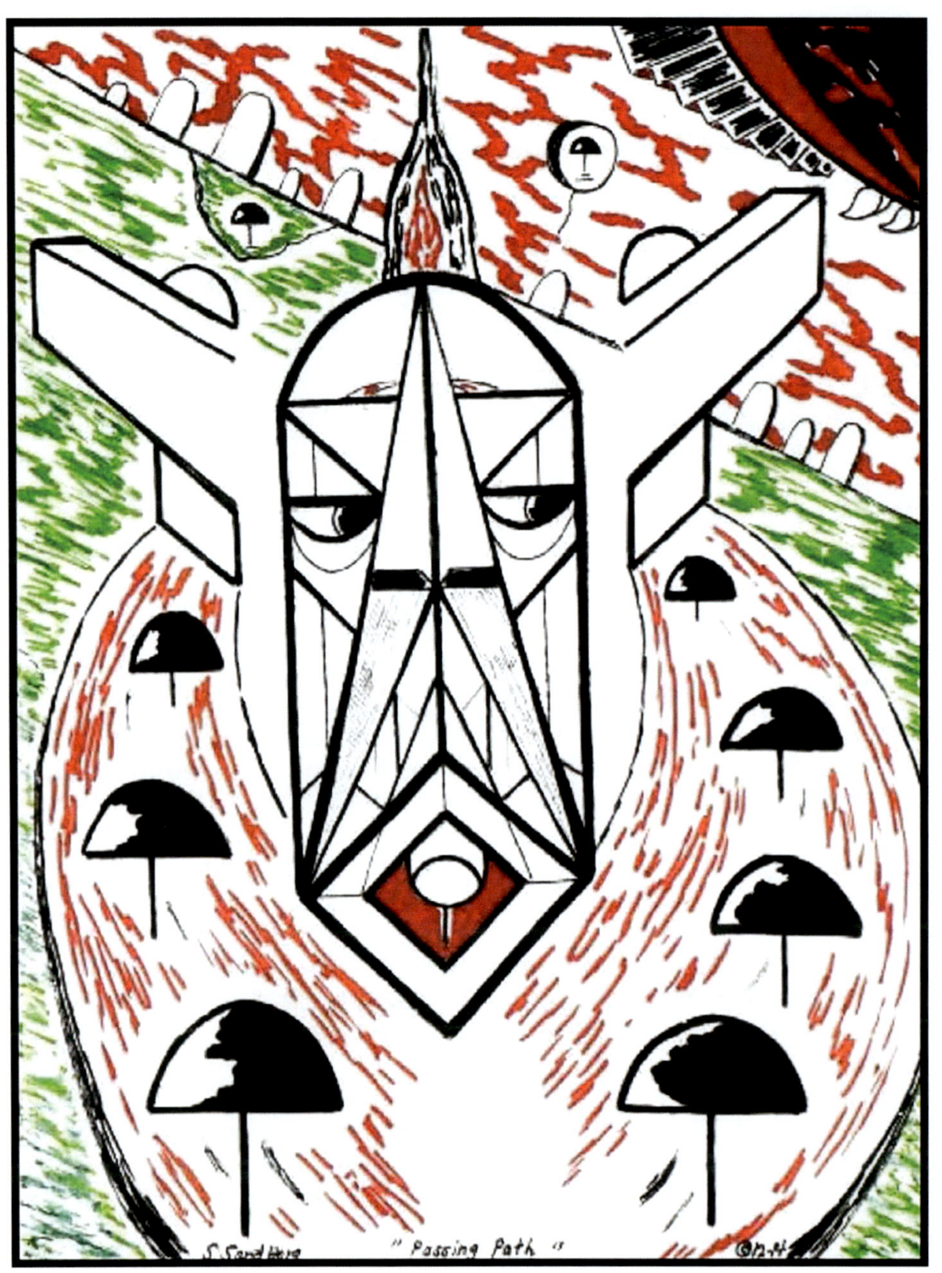

Passing Path

Unfortunately, the road was taken.

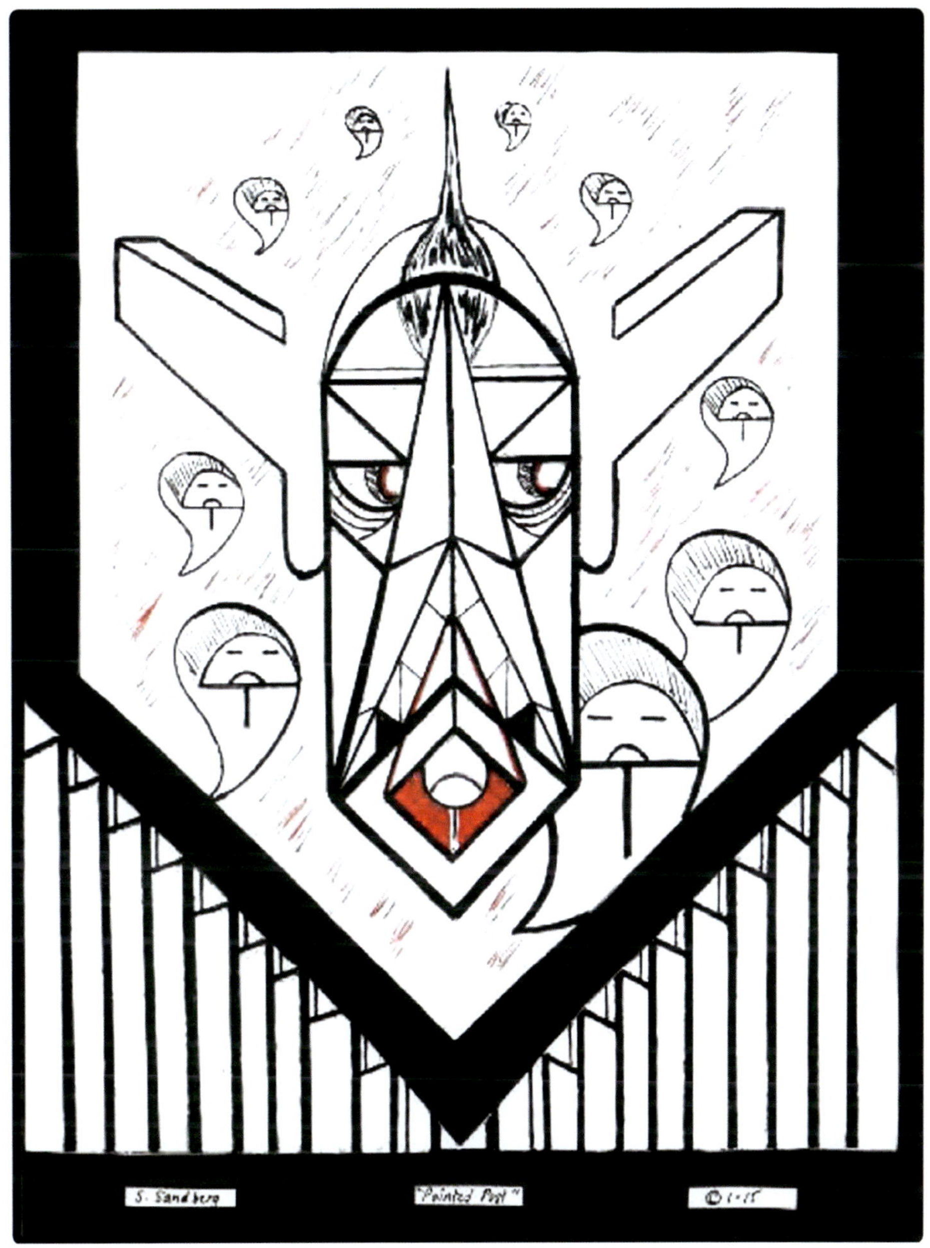

Pointed Post

Memories of 'the event' remain sharp in public consciousness.

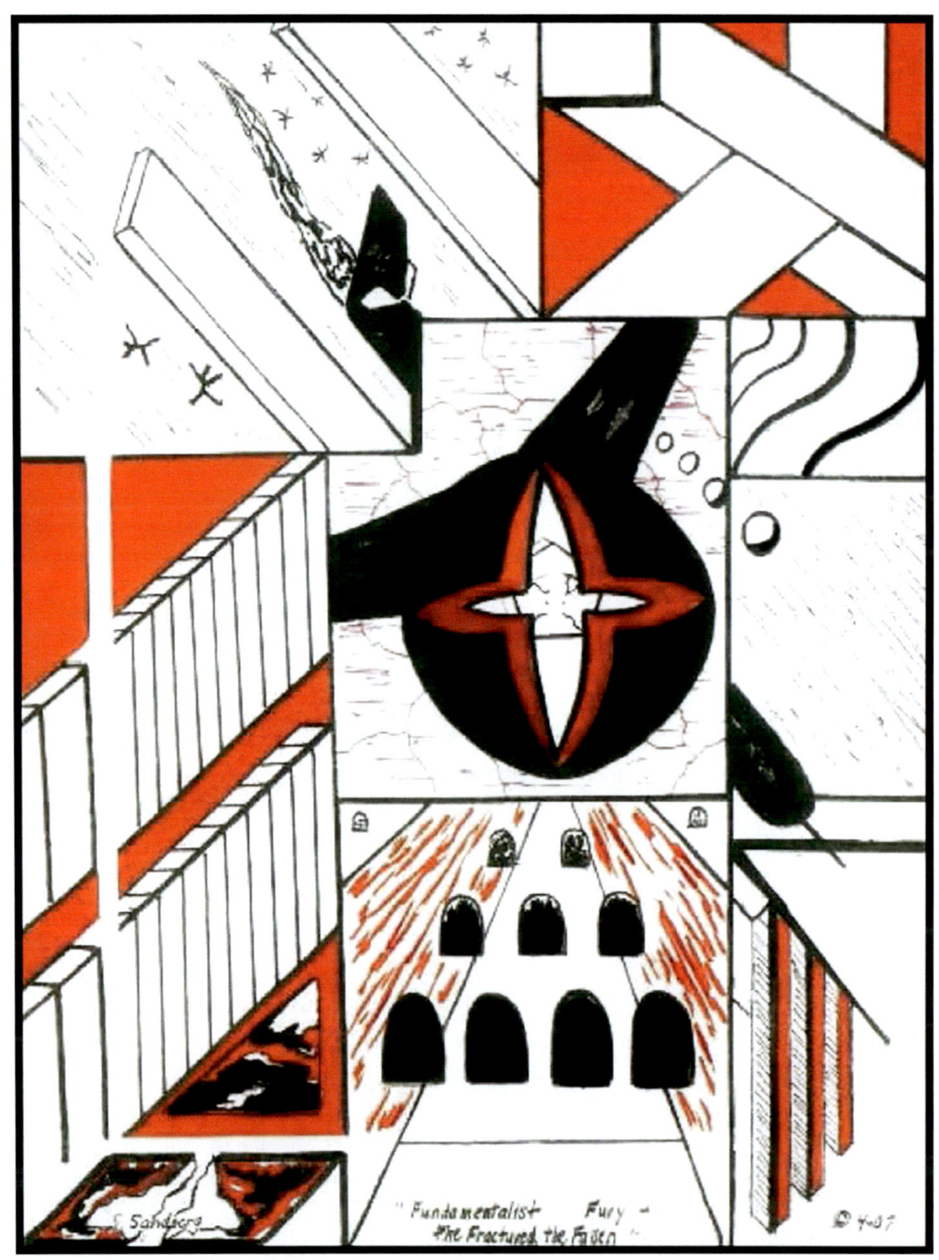

Fundamentalist Fury

Fears remain, the pieces, the sections, never quite make us whole.

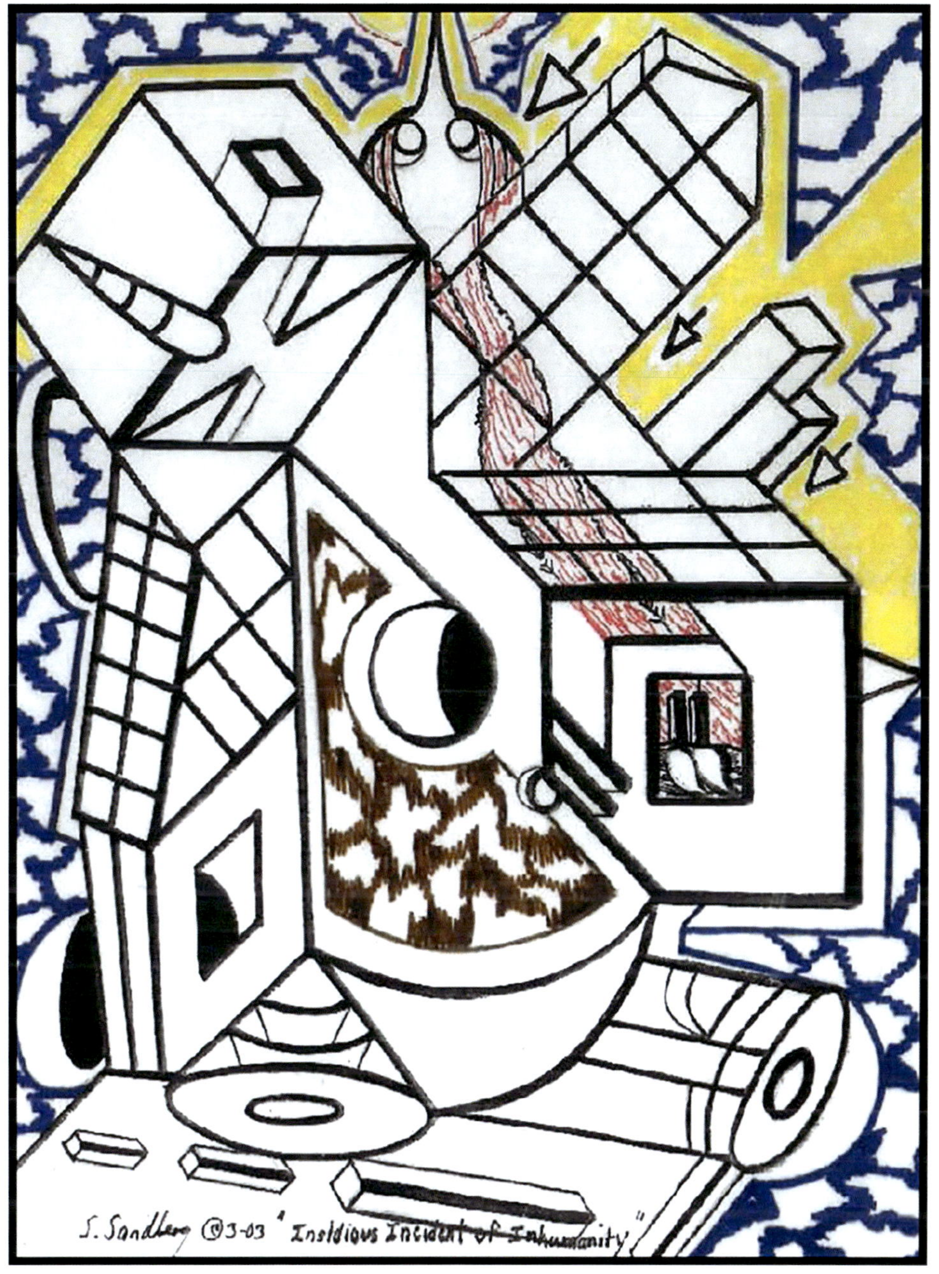

Insidious Incident of Inhumanity

Man's destructive impulses toward his fellow man would
be on full display.

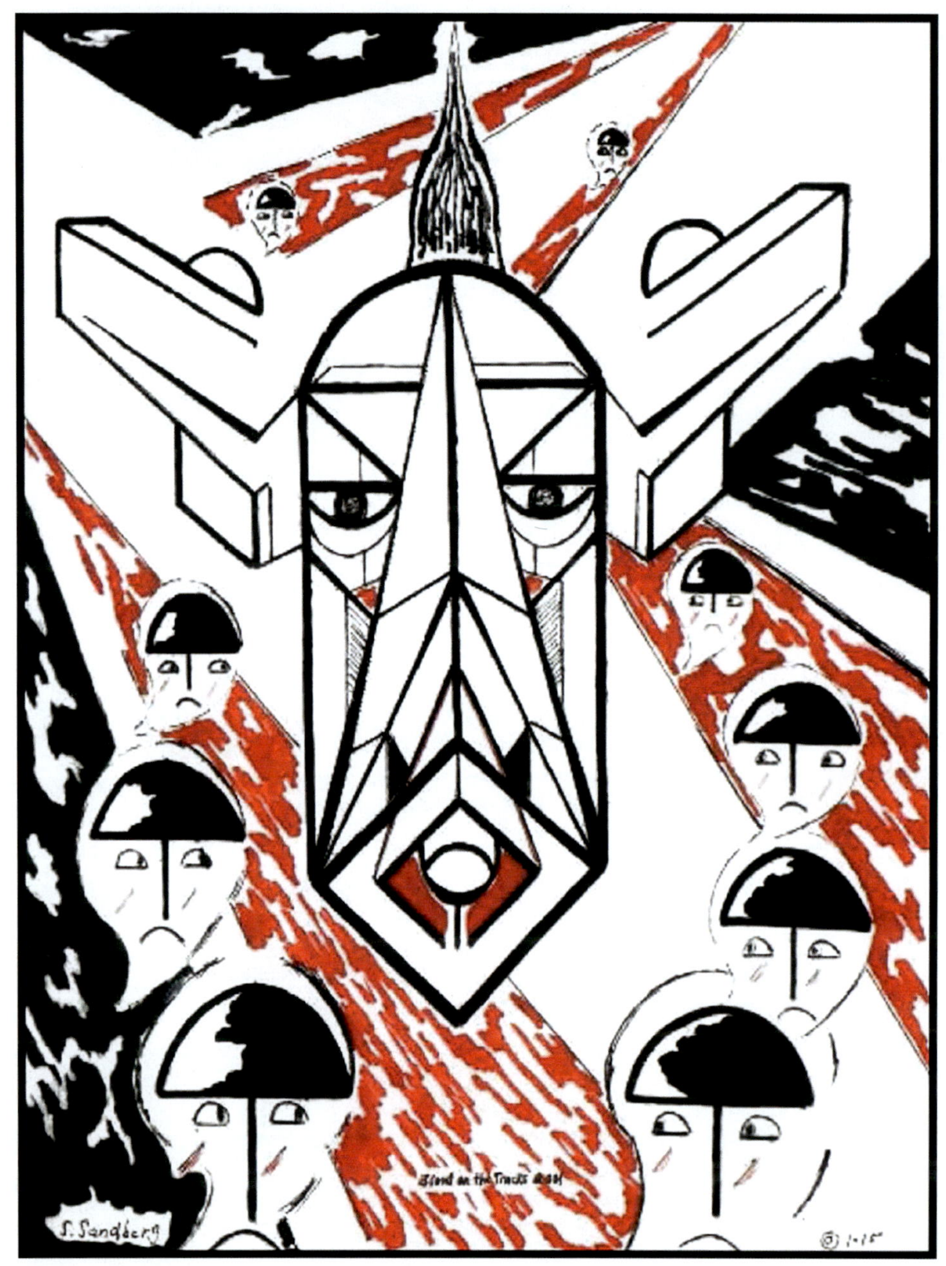

Blood On the Tracks

A path that led to human carnage.

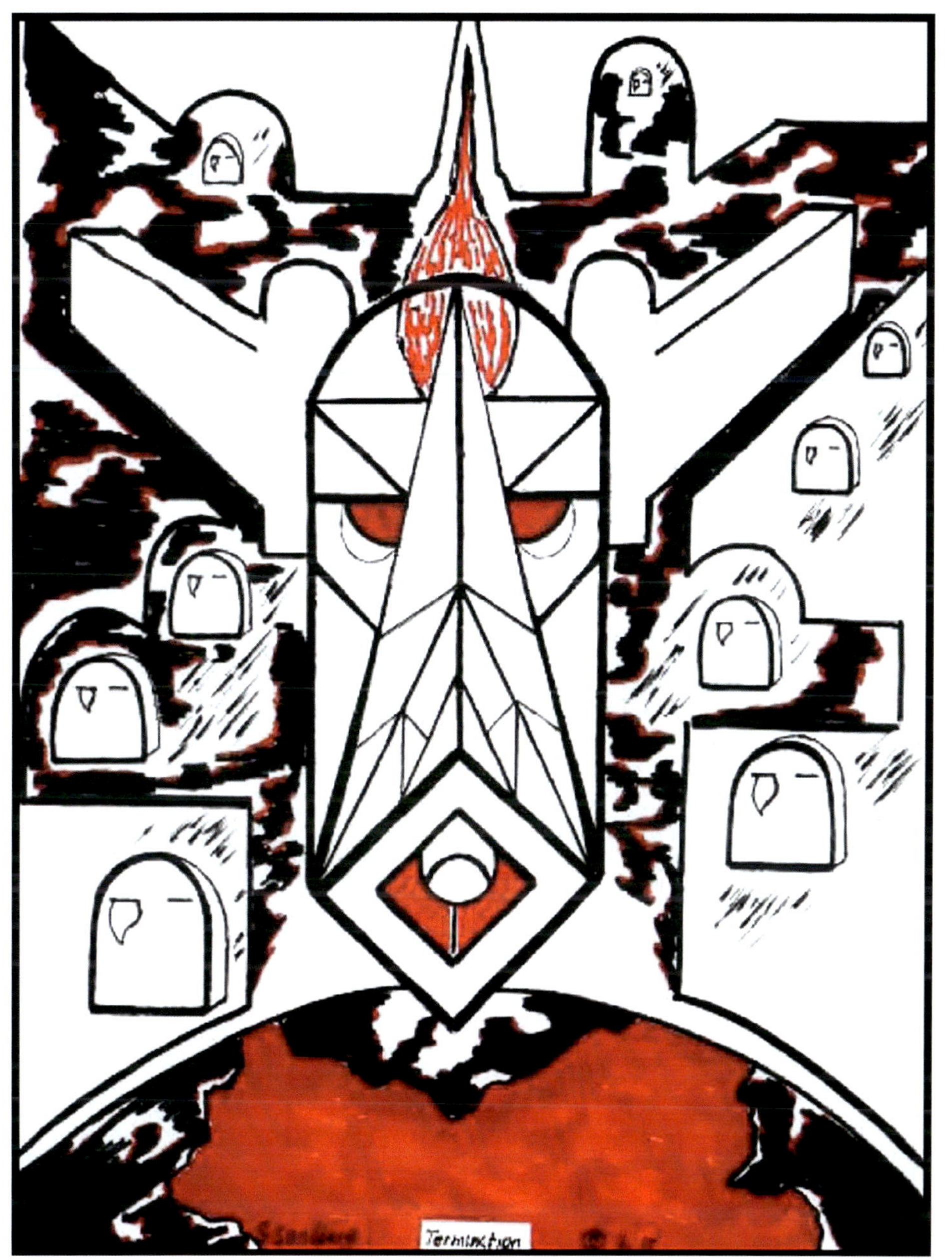

Termination

The End?

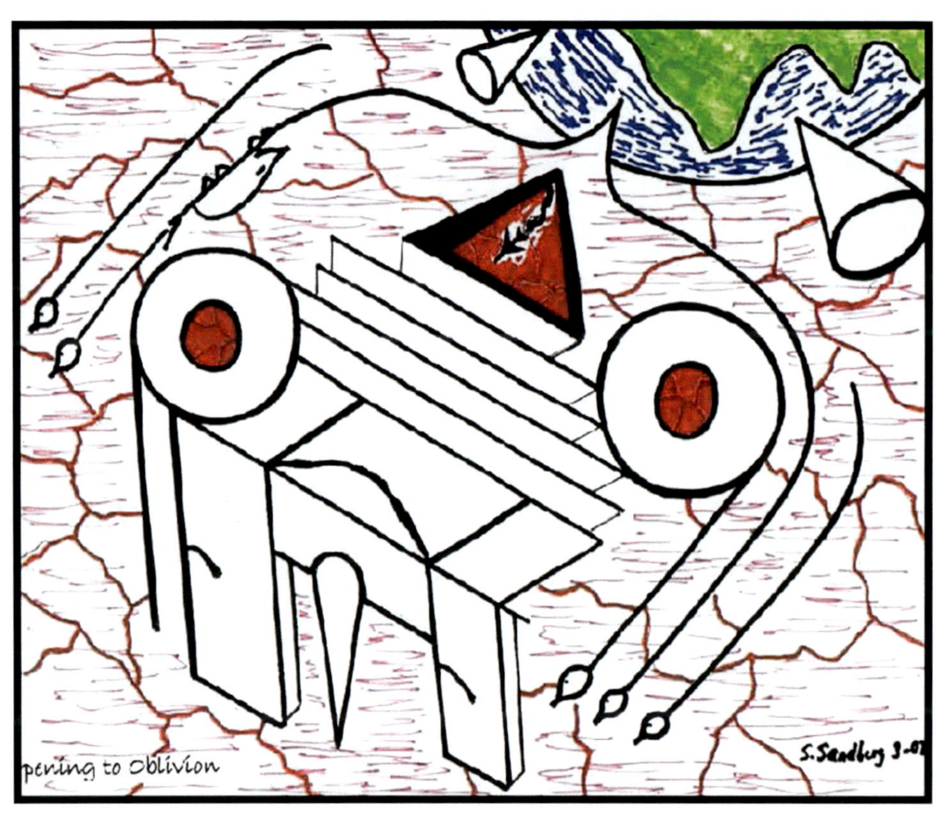

Opening to Oblivion

An ending that was not anticipated; has the final chapter
been written?

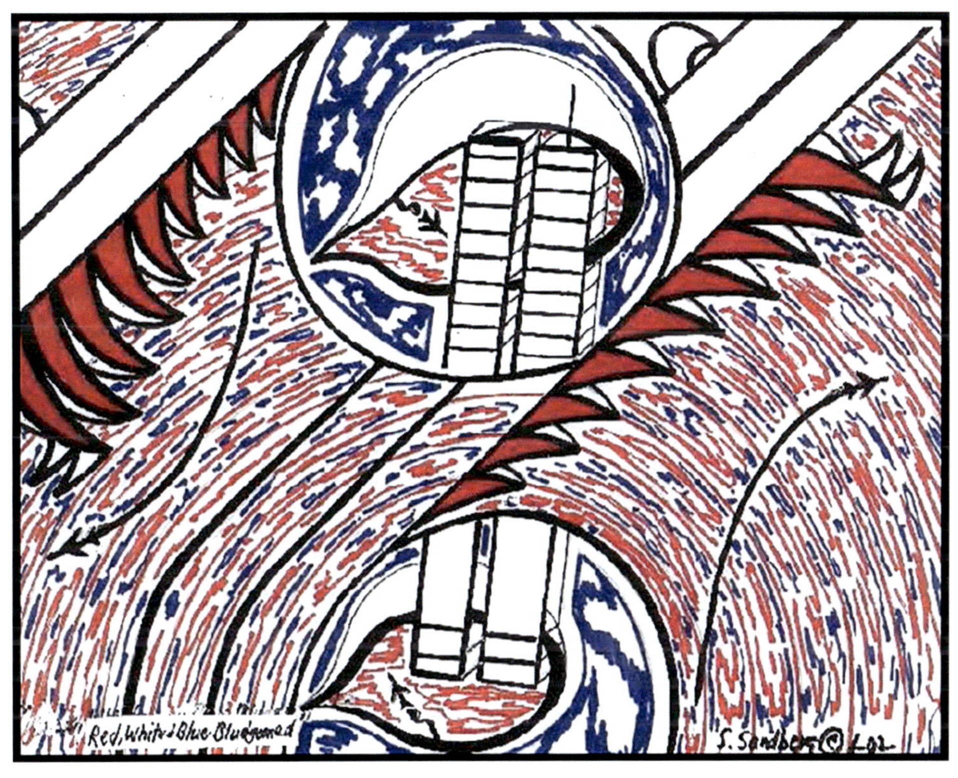

Red, White and Blue Bludgeoned

Our 'colors' had not been attacked beyond our shores in nearly two centuries.

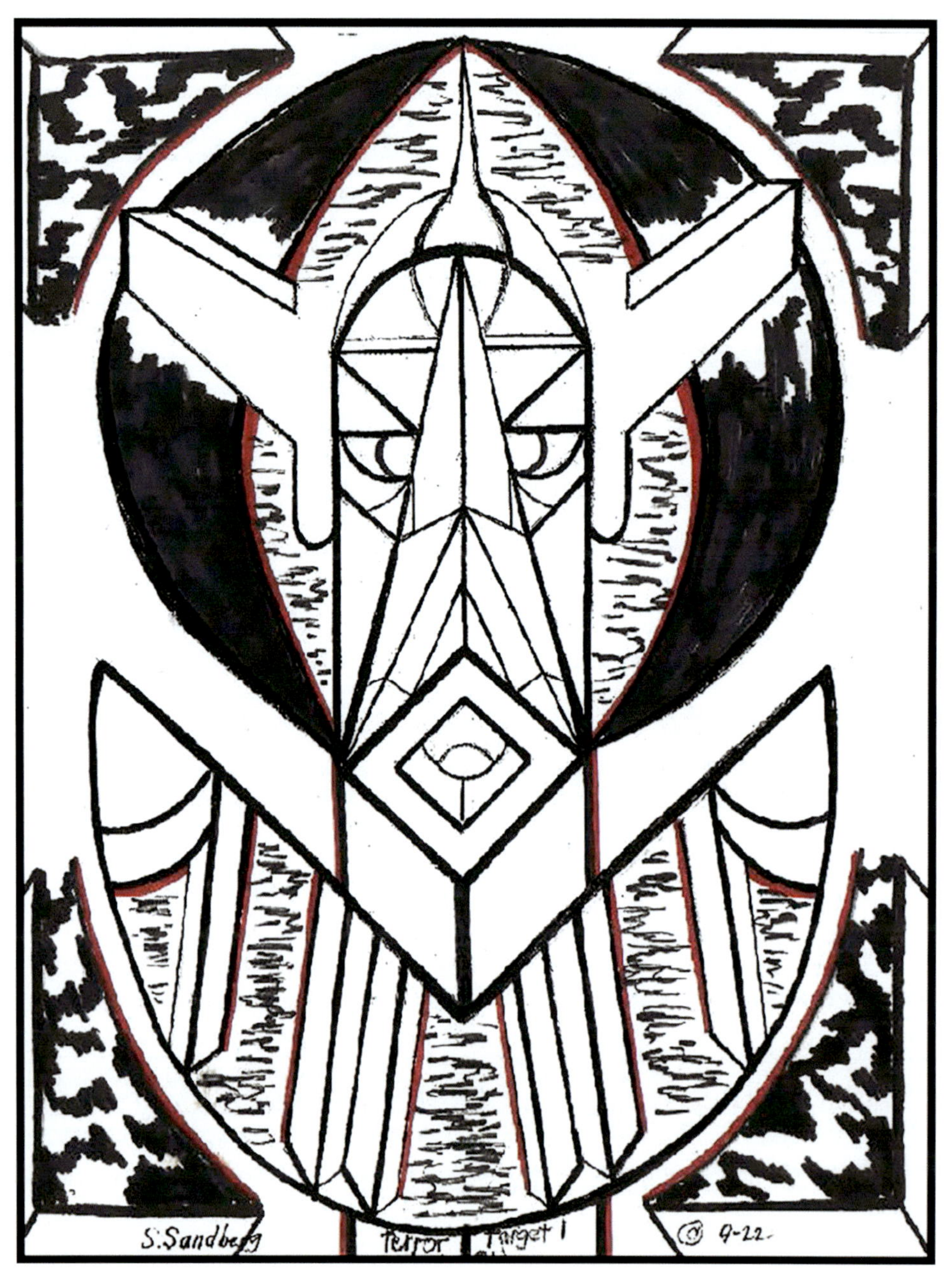

Terror Target (2001)

They took a slice of humanity that day.

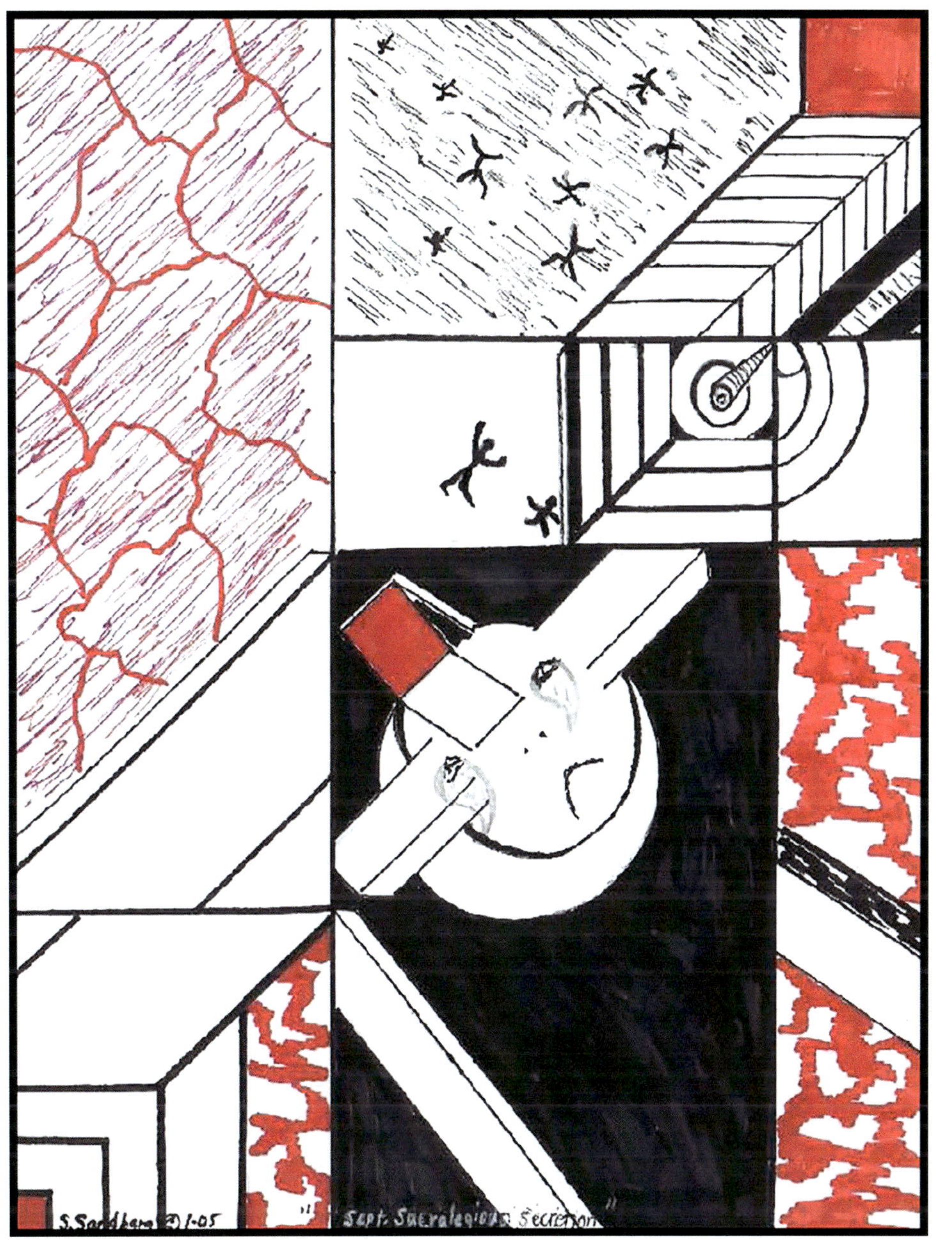

September Sacrilegious Secretion

Religious doctrines are morphed and weaponized into instruments of evil.

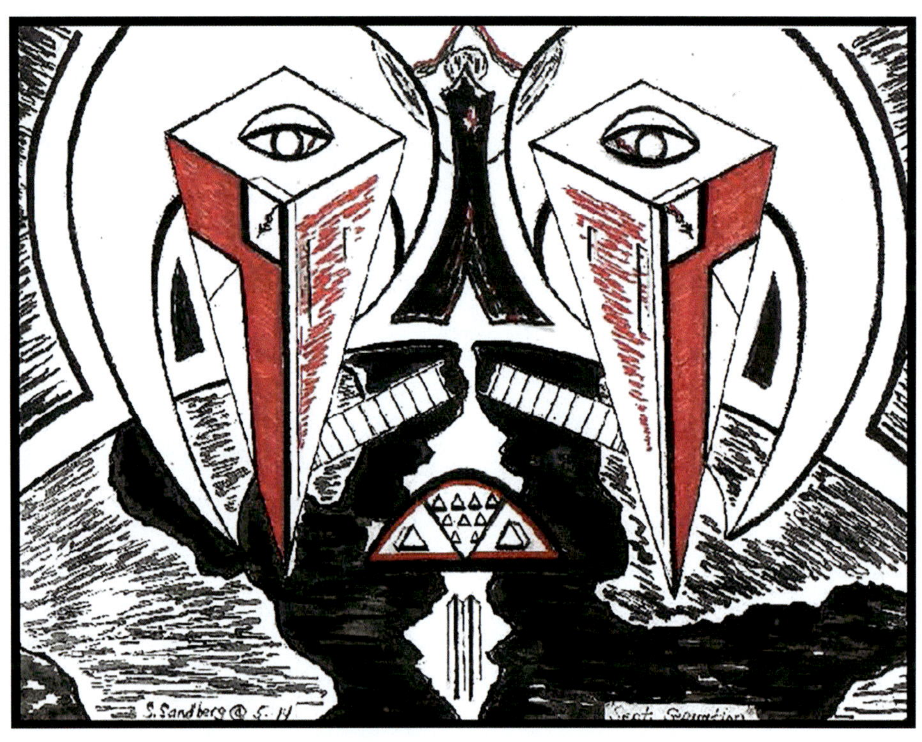

Sept. Separation

Divisions in the world were no more evident than on that day.

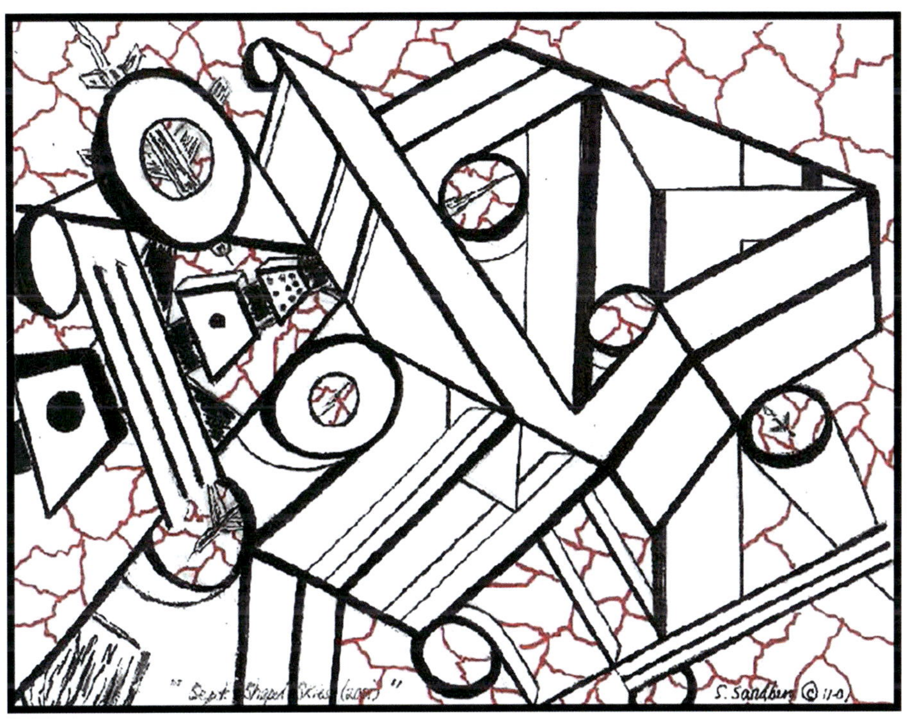

Sept. Shaped Skies

Ultimate horror would soon emanate from the firmament.

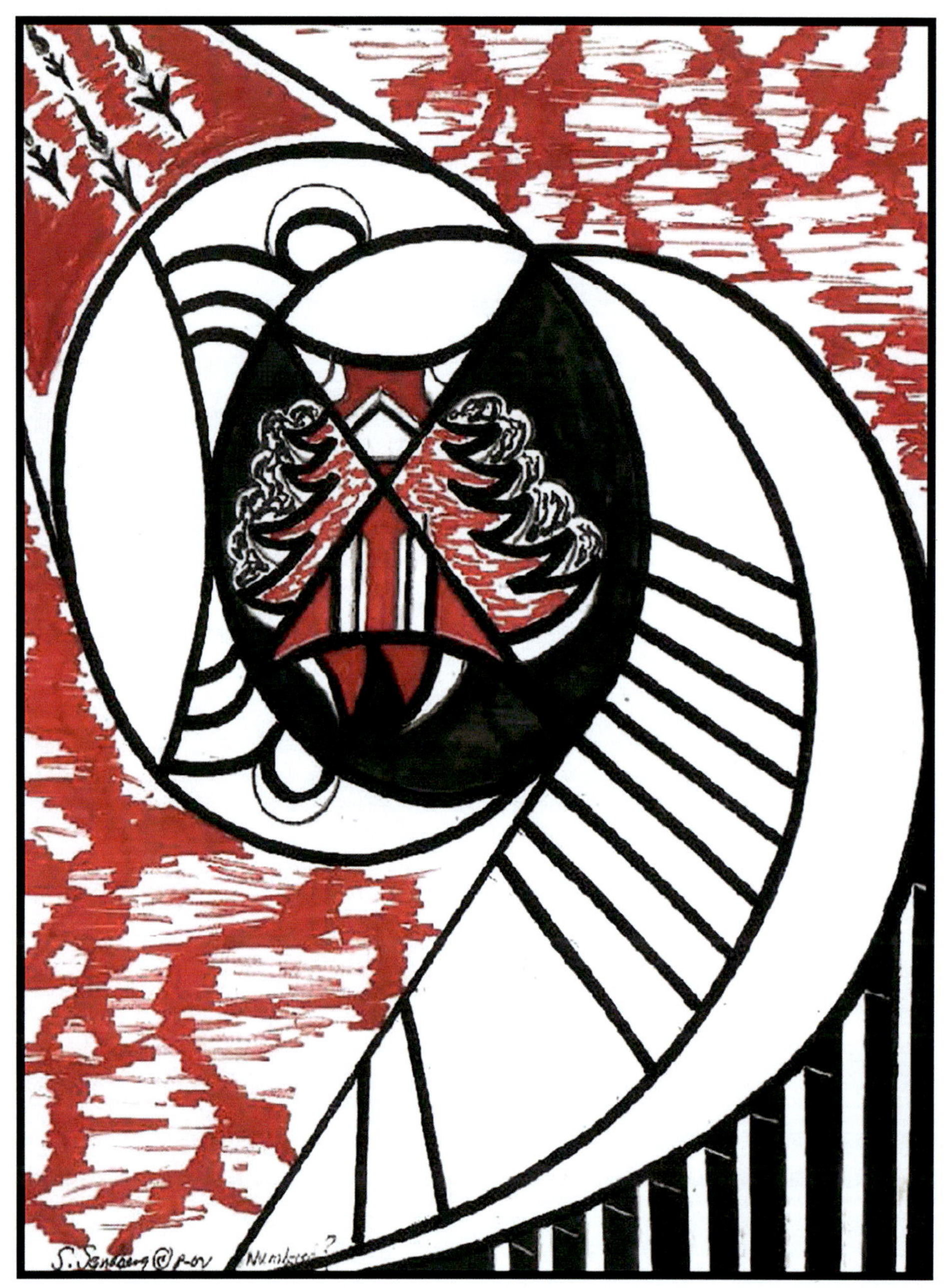

Numbered?

Was 9/11 pre-destined?

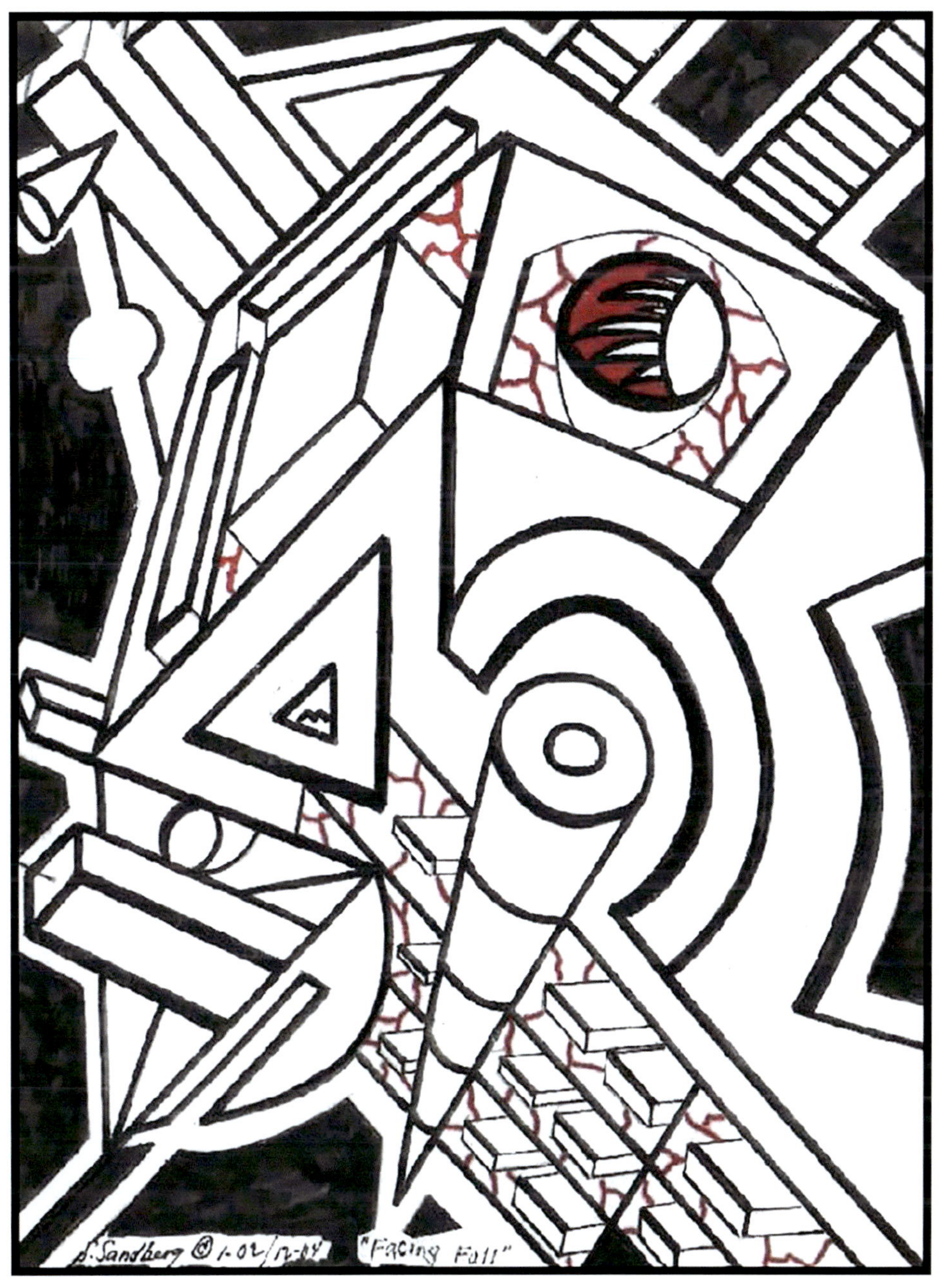

Facing Fall

We would have to face the reality of an uncertain future.

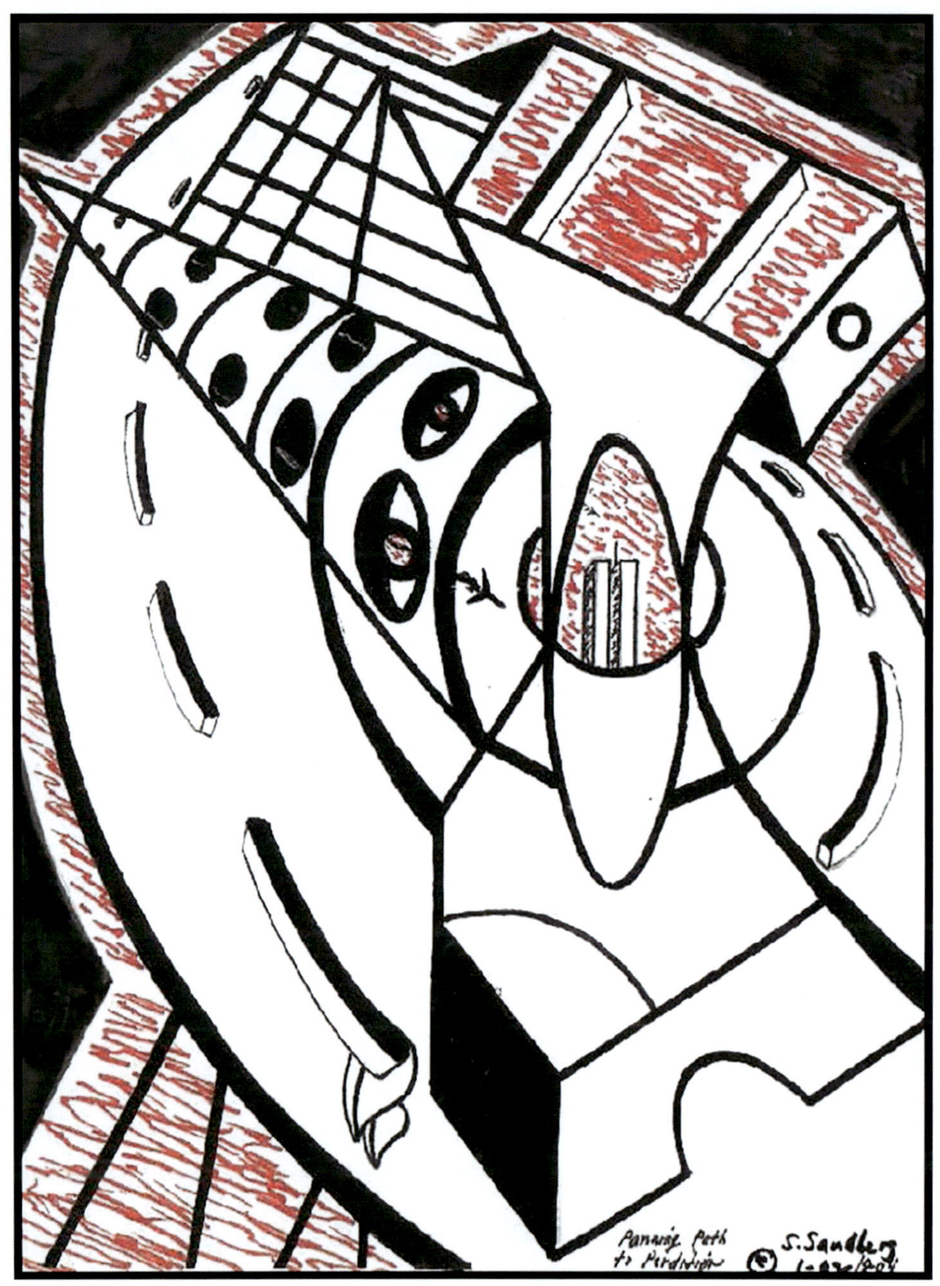

Panning Fall to Perdition

The road to destruction became quite evident by day's end.

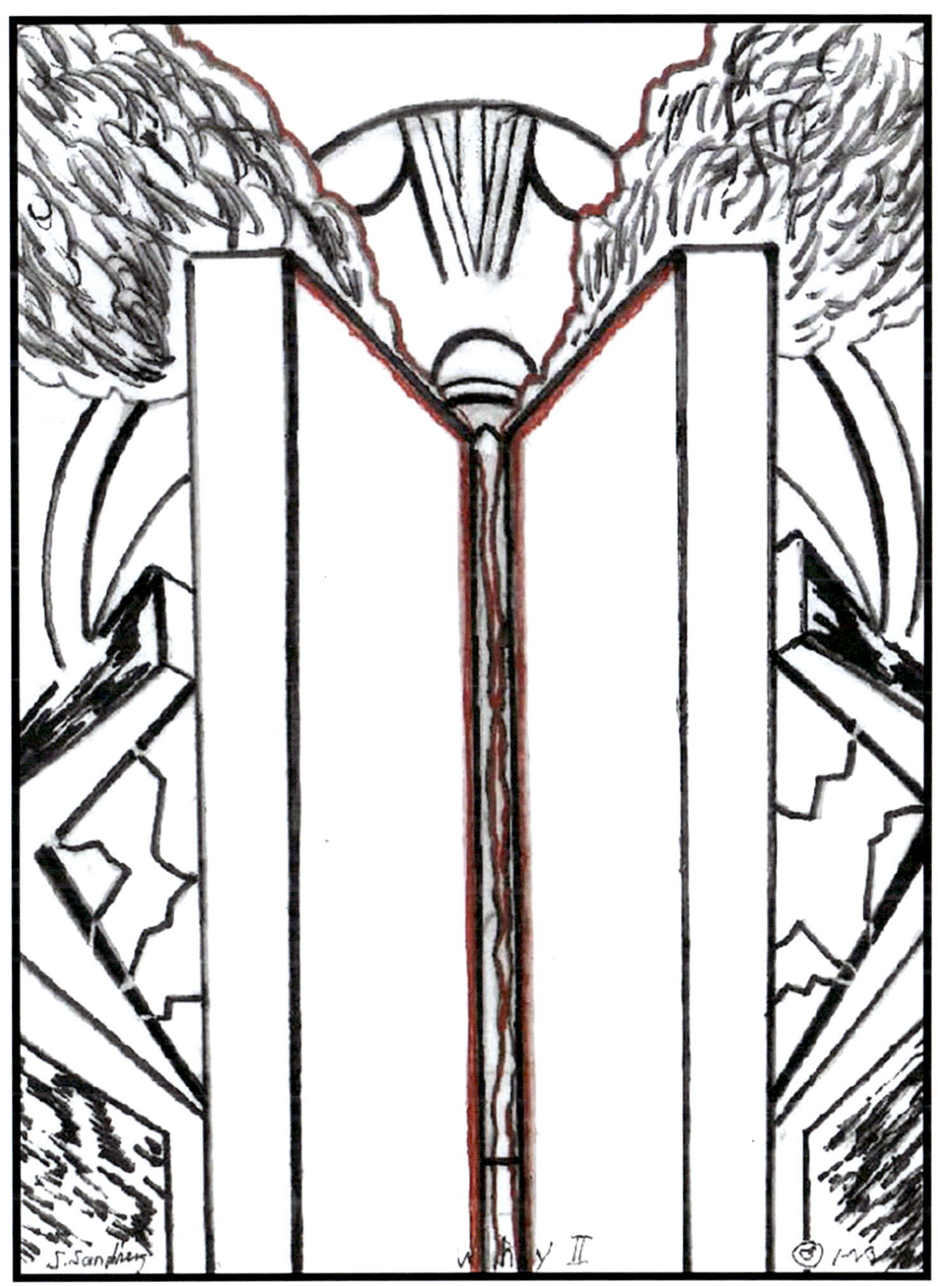

Why II

A Question that soon became answered.

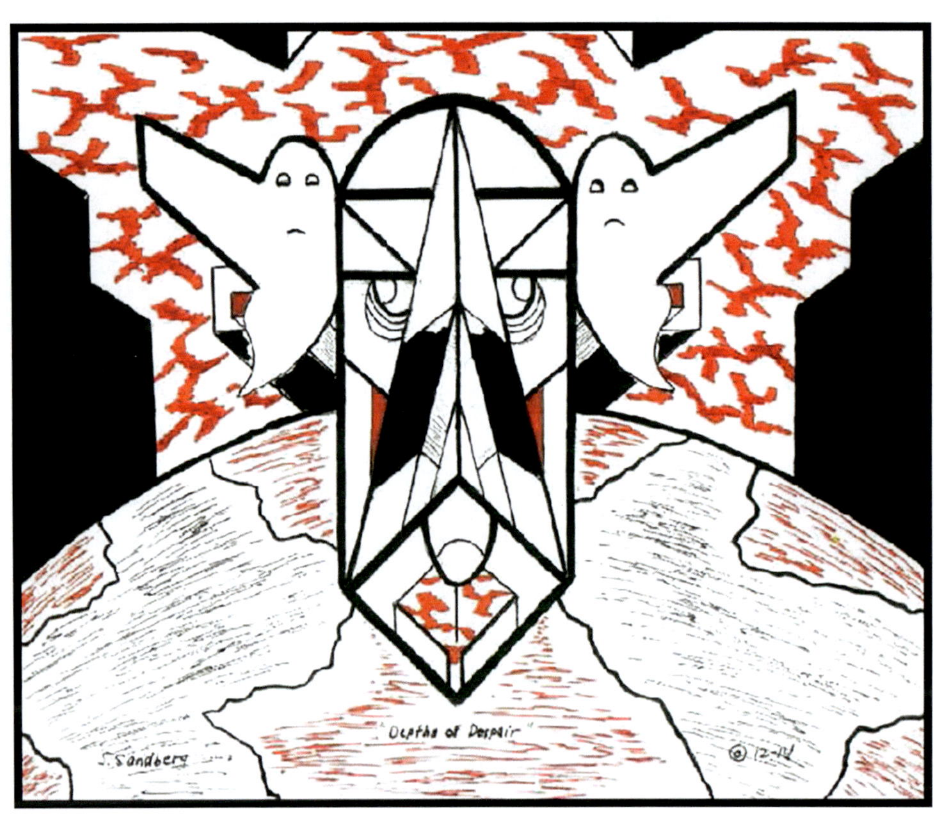

Depths of Despair

A dimension of despondency never quite seen before.

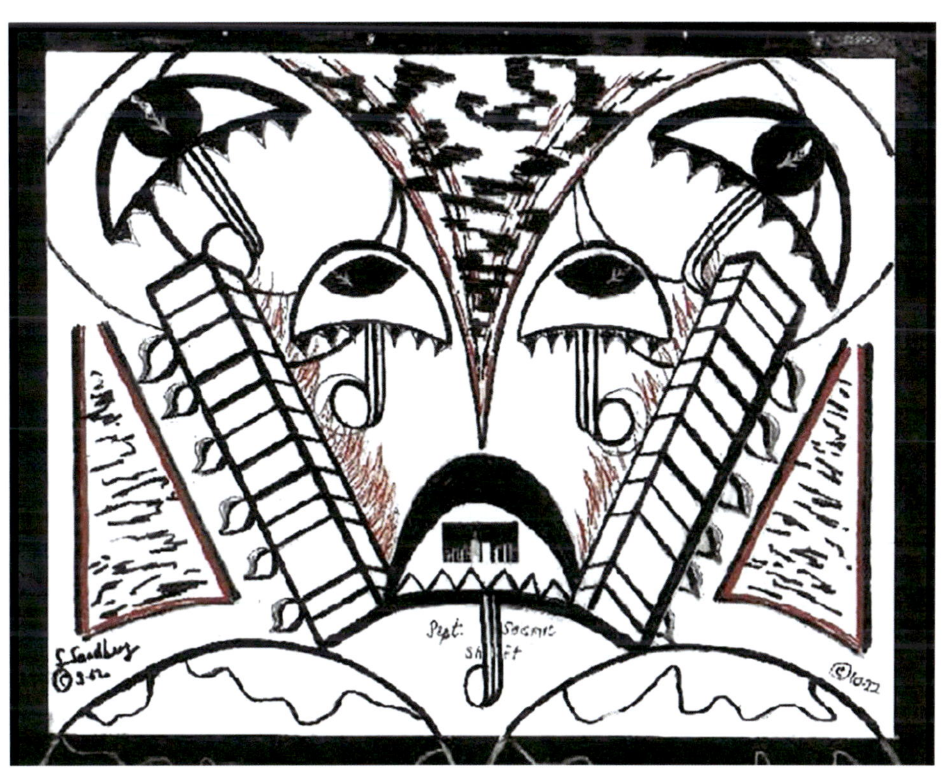

Sept. Seismic Shift

As the towers toppled, our world seemingly came apart.

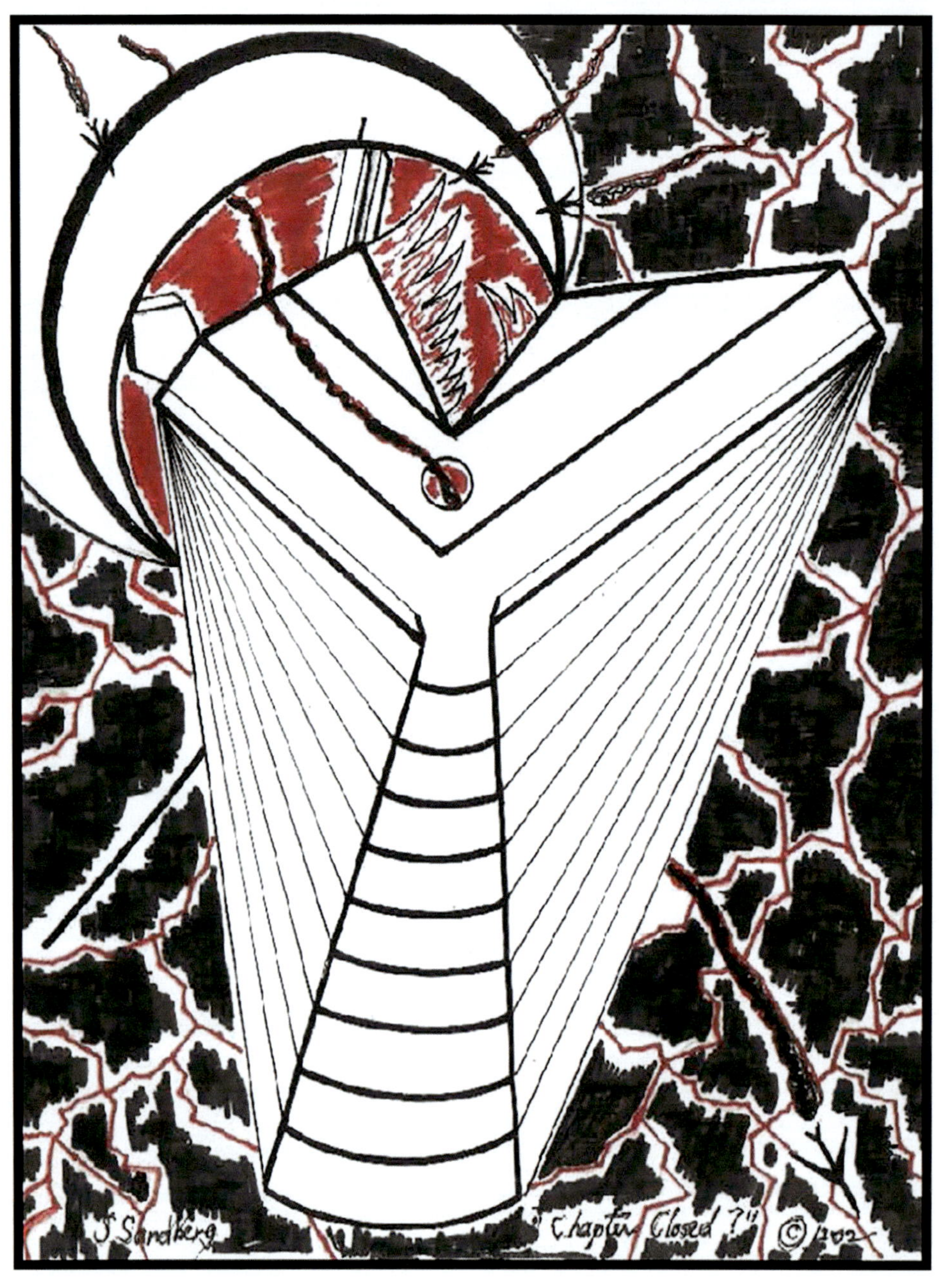

Chapter Closed?

We still must remain vigilant, but maybe we should also peer inward to become more prudent.

THE END